Praise for

"For all who seek to unlock the very real magic within, Tess White-hurst offers not just one key, but an entire golden key ring that opens the sacred mysteries of life and love. A generous and percep-tive book!"

—Sara Wiseman, author of *Messages from the Divine* and *The Intuitive Path*

"Every time I sit down with a book by Tess Whitehurst, I know I'm in for something special, and *You Are Magical* does not disappoint! Tess shows us how to kick things up and find our own magic. Her deep knowledge and radiant love for magic is contagious!"

—Jodi Livon, author of The Happy Medium® book series

YOU ARE
magical

About the Author

Tess Whitehurst teaches magical and intuitive arts in live workshops and via her online community and learning hub, the Good Vibe Tribe Online School of Magical Arts. An award-winning author, she's written eight books, which have been translated into eighteen languages. She has appeared on the Bravo TV show *Flipping Out* as well as morning shows on both Fox and NBC, and her writing has been featured in *Writer's Digest* and *Spirit & Destiny* (in the UK) and on ElephantJournal.com. She lives in the Rocky Mountains near Boulder, CO. Visit her online at TessWhitehurst.com.

Tess
Whitehurst

• • •

YOU ARE
magical

Llewellyn Publications
Woodbury, Minnesota

FIRST EDITION
First Printing, 2018

Cover design by Shira Atakpu and Ellen Lawson
Chakra illustration by Mary Ann Zapalac

Llewellyn Publications is a registered trademark of Llewellyn Worldwide Ltd.

Library of Congress Cataloging-in-Publication Data

Names: Whitehurst, Tess, author.
Title: You are magical / by Tess Whitehurst.
Description: First Edition. | Woodbury : Llewellyn Worldwide, Ltd., 2018. |
    Includes bibliographical references.
Identifiers: LCCN 2018016324 (print) | LCCN 2018023016 (ebook) | ISBN
    9780738756806 () | ISBN 9780738756783 (alk. paper)
Subjects: LCSH: Magic. | Witchcraft. | Occultism.
Classification: LCC BF1611 (ebook) | LCC BF1611 .W66 2018 (print) | DDC
    133.4/3—dc23
LC record available at https://lccn.loc.gov/2018016324

Llewellyn Worldwide Ltd. does not participate in, endorse, or have any authority or responsibility concerning private business transactions between our authors and the public.

All mail addressed to the author is forwarded but the publisher cannot, unless specifically instructed by the author, give out an address or phone number.

Any internet references contained in this work are current at publication time, but the publisher cannot guarantee that a specific location will continue to be maintained. Please refer to the publisher's website for links to authors' websites and other sources.

Llewellyn Publications
A Division of Llewellyn Worldwide Ltd.
2143 Wooddale Drive
Woodbury, MN 55125-2989
www.llewellyn.com

Printed in the United States of America

Other Books by Tess Whitehurst

Magical Housekeeping
(Llewellyn, 2010)

The Good Energy Book
(Llewellyn, 2012)

The Art of Bliss
(Llewellyn, 2012)

The Magic of Flowers
(Llewellyn, 2013)

Magical Fashionista
(Llewellyn, 2013)

Holistic Energy Magic
(Llewellyn, 2015)

Magic of Flowers Oracle
(Llewellyn, 2015)

Llewellyn's Complete Book of Mindful Living (contributor)
(Llewellyn, 2016)

The Magic of Trees
(Llewellyn, 2017)

Forthcoming Books by Tess Whitehurst

The Unicorn Revolution
(Llewellyn, 2019)

Disclaimer

The material in this book is not intended as a substitute for trained medical or psychological advice. Readers are advised to consult their personal healthcare professionals regarding treatment.

Dedication

To the powerful magic within you, the reader. May you wield it with mastery and may it bring waves of joy and wellbeing to you, your loved ones, and the world.

Contents

PART 2: *Working Your Magic*

Preface

A month before I was born, my mom wrote me a letter. While she was going through old stuff a few years ago, she came across it and finally sent it to me.

Every time I read it, it makes me cry. Among many other beautiful things, it says:

> There is so much I want to tell you from my little perch here in space and time. But I'm hoping and believing that what I'm inspired to write now will be what you need to be reading, not what I need to be writing.
>
> Don't be forgetting the magic. You know what I mean. If you don't, you never did, but it's easy to forget. So much magic, like you kicking me from within my body, like me communicating with you now across the years.

There is an infinite number of types of magic, and now there is even one more: your magic. I can't tell you more, but you will know.

Even though I received the letter only recently, I like to think I have been successful at not forgetting the magic. In fact, you might say I've made it my life's work to remember the magic, and to support other people in remembering it too.

Magic has always been a part of my life, but it was just over twenty years ago that I discovered it as a spiritual practice. Since my first book, *Magical Housekeeping*, came out in 2010, I have been publicly writing and teaching about magical living, as well as supporting clients through my intuitive counseling and feng shui work. Now, in this book, I share the fundamentals of living a magical life. It's been shaped by the many questions and concerns I've heard from readers, clients, and students over the years, as well as all that I've learned along my own spiritual and magical path.

Considering you've found your way to this book, it's likely that you're like me, and have a stubborn sense that there is much more going on here than most people publicly discuss: invisible currents of energy, information, and interconnection that inform and define all things. There was a time when I found this sense most unsettling. It was like I was filled with ungrounded electricity, which I believe led to anxiety, depression, and the unwitting creation and maintenance of a host of undesirable life conditions. Discovering magic as a spiritual path provided the perfect remedy by showing me how to harness and channel my awareness of the subtle reality into harmony, healing, and the power to create positive change.

Since that time, my life has been systematically unfolding in more and more magical ways. I am constantly astonished by the relentless expansion of beauty in my world. Although I still encounter challenges, like everyone does, I see even these as opportunities to learn, grow, and expand into even deeper wisdom and power than ever before.

I would love for you to experience what I'm talking about firsthand.

That's why I wrote this book for *you*: you who can no longer ignore the ancient, insistent, mesmerizing siren song of your intrinsic spiritual power. I wrote it for you who can sense that living magically is not a novelty act, a fashion, or a trend; it's who you really are. Indeed, it's your legacy and birthright as a beloved child of the universe. Welcome home.

To borrow the immortal words of my mother, I am pleased to be able to say:

"There is an infinite number of types of magic, and now there is even one more: *your* magic."

PART 1

• • •

Finding Your Magic

1

Answering the Call

Ever since you were a child, magic has called to you.

Even when the grownups told you it was all just make-believe, you could never entirely dismiss the idea that power flows from your fingertips, your dreams carry messages from beyond, and maybe—just maybe—you can adjust, fine-tune, and craft your world to match your desires.

And that idea is still with you today. It may have been buried at times, but at its core it hasn't faded.

What's more, you feel a pulsating power and presence emanating from the natural world. It speaks to you—not necessarily through words, but through the beauty of a butterfly, the fragrance of fresh rain on dry ground, the sound of wind in the trees, the vast expanse of glittering stars, or the moment when the sun shines through rain to broadcast a rainbow.

Even if you've never consciously acknowledged this feeling, now that I've described it, you recognize it plainly. And it's so profound that it's actually spiritual.

But mainstream spirituality—organized or prescribed religion of any variety—has always let you down. Your experience of it has never come close to how transported you feel by your own personal relationship with nature and the cosmos.

Why is all that, do you think?

Well, I'll tell you.

It's because you are magical.

The Mystery Is Sacred

Some Native American tribes have a name for the divine presence that translates to the "Great Mystery" or the "Great Holy Mystery."

While the modern Western world may like a good mystery novel or unsolved crime story, it's a different story with *the* Mystery with a capital *M*. Science and organized religion alike seem to believe it's their mission to explain it all away, to tell us how they're getting it all sorted out, figured out, and written down.

But in our heart of hearts, we know that the Mystery—that relentless "why" at the innermost core of time, space, and existence—is what makes this life what it is. It's a question that can never be answered and a wildness that can never be tamed. It won't shrink itself to fit into the confines of our logical, linear minds. It hides in the tiniest particles, plunges to the deepest depths, and expands extravagantly across the infinite, glittering cosmos. And when we surrender to it and open up to it, our consciousness goes there too.

This is where your magic comes from. And, like the unfathomable depth and breadth of the Great Mystery itself, it's perhaps what has made so many so uncomfortable about metaphysics and the supernatural for so long.

Everything Is Interconnected

While all our logic will never penetrate the heart of the Great Mystery, the fact remains that we and the Great Mystery are one. Relatively recent science describes the quantum interconnectedness of all things: the existence of everything as a unified field of energy. This means that while we are in the universe, the universe is also within us. There is no separation. While science is just beginning to have words for this, it's something that spiritual and magical people have sensed since time immemorial.

In the story of Svetaketu in the Chandogya Upanishad (one of the ancient Sanskrit sacred texts), it is said: "One unbounded ocean of consciousness became light, water, and matter. And the three became many. In this way the whole universe was created as an unbounded ocean of consciousness ever unfolding within itself."

Believe it or not, in the 2006 book *Pride of India*, the quantum mechanics pioneer Werner Heisenberg is quoted as saying, "After the conversations about Indian philosophy, some of the ideas of quantum physics that had seemed so crazy suddenly made much more sense."

The classic magical text known as *The Kybalion* also foreshadowed the quantum perspective. In chapter 4 it states, "[The All] must be infinite in space—it must be everywhere, for there is no place outside of the All." So not only are we created by what the Kybalion calls the "All," but we are also made up of it: we are extensions of it. We contain it within us. Similarly, Erwin Schrödinger, the Austrian theoretical physicist famous for his contributions to quantum mechanics, writes in his book *My View of the World* that "inconceivable as is seems to ordinary reason, you—and all other conscious beings as such—are all in all. Hence, this life of yours … is in a certain sense the whole."

Even the most limited understanding of our physical existence illustrates how much we rely on food, water, air, and other beings. Without these things, we literally would not exist. The genetic material of our parents, the food we eat, the water we drink, and the air we breathe become us, as even our own atoms and molecules will inevitably become something else. Where and when does one end and the other begin? The answers, of course, are *nowhere* and *never*: there is no separation—no beginning and no end.

Clearly, you are one with the All, the power that creates and sustains worlds. That power is not separate from you. It belongs to you. It *is* you. And if magic is the power to create positive change according to your will and desires, well, then, there's no denying it: *you are magical.*

You Are Magical

Once you recognize and admit that you are magical—that you are one with the vast power that creates everything—you're empowered to wield your magic. It becomes possible to shape your world according to your will: to live the life and create the conditions you desire.

But magic's first gift is its best gift, and that is simply the awareness that you have it, that it's yours. In other words, through consciously connecting with the Great Mystery and allowing yourself to recognize your oneness with the unified field, your life instantly becomes animated with beauty, meaning, and wonder. Everything else—all the crafting and shaping of your life conditions according to your desires—is just (impossibly delicious) icing on the cake.

This book is about the cake *and* the icing: the luminous, wondrous, profound awareness of the Mystery and all the fun ways you can channel it into continuously creating the life of your dreams.

After all, you're meant to live a magical life: a life filled with beauty, wonder, and power.

But you already knew that, didn't you? You were born knowing. And it's worth noting that all the anti-Mystery propaganda the world has offered you over the years—try as it might—has never quite succeeded in convincing you otherwise.

Your Magic Is Unique to You

Every musician's music has its own unique expression and aesthetic signature. Your magic is no different. While all creativity and all magic come from the same unified field, just as everything does, the particular emanations—much like our fingerprints and DNA—are infinitely varied.

To make contact with your magic and to begin to familiarize yourself with its unique expression, ask yourself: What inspires me? What excites me? What connects me to the Mystery, to Mother Nature, to All That Is?

With this in mind, here are some journaling questions to help you open the door to your magical path:

1. What is your favorite flower, or what flowers are particularly beautiful and inspiring to you?

2. What is your favorite tree, or what trees are particularly beautiful and inspiring to you?

3. What is your favorite animal, or what animals are particularly beautiful and inspiring to you?

4. Why did you choose these flowers, trees, and animals? What emotions do you feel when you spend time with them, see them, or call them to mind? What messages do they give you? How might these messages and feelings be significant to

your present life experience? What do they show you about yourself? Devote time and attention to each one individually.

5. What speaks to your sense of divine connection, or what most aligns you with a feeling of profound spiritual inspiration? It could be a particular god or goddess, an entire spiritual tradition, yoga, a story, crystals, a mythological creature, science, poetry, a country, a historical period, herbal healing, a specific scent or herb, an aspect of the earthly environment, the stars, space, or anything else. List as many as you like.

6. Why did you choose the answers you did for the previous question? What is it about these things that speaks to you, or what feelings do they give you? How might these feelings or qualities be significant to your present life experience? What do they show you about yourself? Take your time with each one.

While the following chapters will explore specifics about how to access and utilize your magic, it's wonderful to begin by simply making contact with it: to appreciate it and revel in it for its own sake. And that which inspires you—which speaks to your sense of mystery and excitement—provides an instant portal to your expansive landscape of potent personal power.

In addition to acting as your very own guideposts to the Great Mystery and all the power and magic it contains, your answers to the previous questions provide clues to your life's purpose as well as the unique magical objects, spell ingredients, symbols, and visualizations that will best serve your magical work, now and throughout your lifetime.

Do keep in mind that just as the seasons and weather change from month to month and year to year, that which inspires you, excites you, and connects you to the realm of the Divine will change regularly and throughout your lifetime. That's part of what makes magic such a vibrant spiritual path: like nature itself, it asks us to stay awake to our ever-changing passion for and ever-deepening relationship with the world and universe around us.

In each chapter in part 1, you'll find one or more exercises to help you integrate and experience what you've learned. Here is the first.

·········· · · · · · · · · · · · ·· YOUR MAGIC ·· · · · · · · · · · · · ·· · · ·····

Answer the Call

*My new awareness of the Goddess spilled over as a new aware-
ness of trees and landscapes, so that what had seemed matter of
fact and dull now began to vibrate with sentience. I would find
myself staring up at a eucalyptus tree as if it were a lover, or
looking out over a landscape with the feeling that it was alive and
breathing.*

~ SALLY KEMPTON, *AWAKENING SHAKTI*

Now that you've connected with your magic, are you ready to answer the call?

- Turn off your phone and spend time alone in an inspiring, relaxing natural setting. This can be a park or nature trail, but it can also be your patio or yard, as long as it's somewhere that inspires you and someplace where you can see plants and the sky.

- Do whatever you like: walk, sit on a tree stump, recline on the grass, gaze at a flower or tree, or watch the clouds. The important thing is that you are consciously present with the natural world around you.

- As you focus your awareness on the alive, conscious wisdom of nature, announce your commitment to answer the call: to live your authentic identity as a magic worker. You can speak your commitment aloud or think it silently. Either way, the Great Mystery and the entire natural world will "hear" and understand the energy behind your words. Don't worry about saying anything formal. Just speak the words that authentically bubble up from your belly and heart.

- Take some time afterward to listen deeply to the wisdom of the Mystery and the natural world. Do you see anything that sparks a deeper understanding? Does anything about the landscape stand out to you? Does any guidance or inspiration seem to magically pop into your head?

- When you get home, write anything in your journal that feels significant to your magical unfolding.

2

Knowing the Legacy

In our culture, magic workers are often called "witches." (Indeed, some magical people proudly identify as such, and you may be one of them.) You may have noticed that the connotations of the word are not always positive. When it isn't used as an insult to describe a not very nice woman, it still carries shades of intimidation or outright evil. Fictional depictions of witches commonly alternate between sexually repulsive and sexually corrupt. It's notable that as our collective consciousness shifts, more recent depictions have evolved. Harry Potter, for example, shows witches as appearing in all shapes, sizes, and moral orientations.

While magic workers and witches can of course be any gender, the archetypal witch—as mythologized in the Western world—is female. When most people think of a wizard, for example, they think of a wise, helpful being like Gandalf or Merlin, not someone who is going to seduce them, steal their baby, or turn them into a frog.

Why the discrepancy? What makes your average mythological witch so different from your average mythological wizard?

Perhaps both illustrate how comfortable our culture is with people who wield large amounts of power. Obviously there is a big difference between our culture's collective degree of comfort with women who wield power and men who do so.

But it goes beyond physical gender. The powers possessed by the witch—healing, intuition, creativity, cooperation, cultivating beauty and harmony, honoring the Mystery, and communicating with the natural world—are traditionally seen as feminine in nature. And as vastly important as all of these are for the sustenance of our planet and wellbeing of our species, they have not been as valued in our culture as what are seen as more masculine strengths, things like science, logic, engineering, war, competition, politics, and commerce.

Now is the time for this to change.

Because only when the polarities come to balance and complement each other—when they work together in harmony within us as individuals and throughout the collective consciousness—will sustainable wellbeing become possible on a global scale. I believe that's why the magical path is calling to so many of us right now.

The Salem Story

Perhaps nothing has shaped our modern concept of witchcraft (and magic) quite like the Salem witch trials. Under intense pressure to do so, the accused spun tales of cavorting with the devil, flying on broomsticks, and selling their souls for worldly luxuries. While there were indeed folk traditions that diverged from the rigid form of Christianity practiced in Salem at that time, the expectations and suspicions of the accusers had a powerful influence on our cultural mythos, both past and present. The shocking series of events was also indicative of something already at work in the collective consciousness: a profound institutionalized mistrust of intuition, sexuality, and a personalized experience of spiritual power.

During the trials, innocent people were hung or pressed to death. Others died in a dark, horrifically unsanitary, overpopulated prison that baked in the summer and literally froze in the winter. An accused child lived in that prison for over a year. A baby was born and died there, never having seen the outside world.

With all of this in mind, one would think these tragic events would lead to a deep mistrust of judges, clergy, and the church in general. Instead, a stubborn vilification of witchcraft is what remains. To this day, hundreds of years later, many parents and religious authority figures in our culture still caution children against practicing witchcraft (or any practices they believe may fall in the same category, such as reading tarot cards or performing nature rituals), believing that it will open them up to spiritual possession and eventually send them to hell.

For example, while in many ways my mother taught me to perceive the world through a magical lens, she has also always adhered to a Christian path and harbored a certain fear of possession. (I suspect this stems from a combination of her Catholic school upbringing and the movie *The Exorcist*.) At around the age of eight, she warned me that things like meditating or mind reading could "open you up to demonic possession," but also that merely *thinking* about Satan gives him power over you. Needless to say, this was like saying, "Whatever you do, don't think about an elephant." I became obsessed with the threat of possession, demons, and hell. I couldn't get them out of my head. I began having terrifying nightmares. While she was just relaying what *she* had been taught, and I'm sure it wasn't her intention to be abusive, such teachings certainly seem to act on the consciousness in an emotionally abusive way.

Beyond Salem

What happened in Salem was a supercharged microcosm of what took place across Europe from the 1500s to the 1700s, when so many of those suspected of witchcraft—or really anything other than the officially sanctioned version of Christianity—were imprisoned, tortured, burned, drowned, and generally terrorized in every way imaginable. It is astounding to consider that organized Christianity instigated this prolonged period of unrelenting horror and went on to enjoy sustained popularity while Witchcraft still hasn't shaken its stigma.

You might say that church officials were seeking (and still seek) to own the spiritual experience, which was once the birthright of all people. Political leaders and church officials alike have systematically chosen to pilfer the spiritual experience from the masses so that it can, presumably, be reached only through recognizing and bowing to their authority.

Speaking of stealing the power that is the birthright of all humans, perhaps nothing is more intrinsically empowering than confidently and comfortably owning one's own sexuality. So it's no wonder fostering guilt and shame around sexuality continues to be a favorite strategy of oppressive organizations all over the world.

The Conversion of the Roman Empire

Going back even further, in the fourth century CE, Constantine forcibly ejected polytheism and established Christianity as the official religion of the Roman Empire (and then moved the capital from Rome to Constantinople, naming it after himself). While this might be because he was a true believer in Christianity, it would also be accurate to say that monotheism was far more philosophically aligned with his grab for absolute power than was polytheism. In addition to its more widely distributed power structure among the various deities, polytheism allows for much more personalization.

In 325 CE, Constantine commissioned the Council of Nicaea to canonize the Bible. In other words, it was the council's job to decide what got thrown out of the Bible and what stayed in. The council then systematically removed the Gnostic texts and many of the books (such as the Gospel of Thomas) that alluded to spiritual power and authority being within the individual rather than requiring a sanctioned intermediary such as the church.

It was also around this time that artistic depictions of Jesus began to portray a white man rather than a Middle Eastern one. More specifically, they began to look a lot like Emperor Constantine himself. Indeed, to this day, when most of us picture Jesus, we are almost certainly not picturing someone who looks like the historical Jesus. Rather, we are picturing someone with a suspiciously strong resemblance to Emperor Constantine.

Let me be clear: by describing this forced shift to monotheism, I don't mean to imply that polytheists were or are morally superior to Christians. In fact, before Constantine, many Christian martyrs suffered a terrible fate at the hands of Roman pagans. What I *do* mean to imply is that the ascendancy of monotheism was in many ways due to political expedience—essentially a justification of one ruler holding absolute power—rather than any sort of intrinsic supremacy of the philosophy.

It's notable that to this day, Western world leaders subscribe almost exclusively to the most popular monotheistic religion of their country. For example, despite the supposed separation of church and state and the fact that one's personal creed should not be involved in the running of a country, every US president up until this writing has quite publicly advertised their allegiance to some form of mainstream Christianity.

The Original Spirituality

For the vast majority of the time that humans have been alive on earth, a magical and shamanic cosmology was the way of the world. This is true for every human culture on the planet. Magic is our heritage. You might say that an awareness of our interconnectedness with all of nature is much more intrinsic to our DNA than is the artificially imposed separation that is the norm in both religious and secular philosophies.

While world shamanic and magical spiritual traditions are endlessly diverse, the following is a brief sample of the countless mystical traditions associated with each continent (except Antarctica, where we are not currently aware of any historical indigenous populations).

Africa

Yoruba, Zulu, and Igbo are just a few of Africa's languages and ethnic groups. Each features a traditional spirituality with a profound reverence for nature, a focus on holistic wellbeing, and a connection with ancestors. In a 2015 interview in *The Harvard Gazette*, Jacob Olupona, Harvard professor of African and African American Studies, notes that "African spirituality simply acknowledges that beliefs and practices touch on and inform every facet of human life, and therefore African religion cannot be separated from the everyday or mundane."

The presence of the pyramids attests to the fact that ancient Egypt possessed highly sophisticated spiritual and scientific technologies. Ancient Egyptian cosmology focused on rebirth, sacred geometry, and the power of numbers, symbols, and words.

Asia

The Hindu religion features a complex, diverse pantheon of divinities that represent various aspects of the human experience. These divinities are invoked and petitioned for various purposes with chanting, altars, and symbols.

Taoism is an energetic, holistic technology that empowers those who study it to create harmony and balance in body, mind, spirit, and home. It counsels an awareness of masculine and feminine energies as well as the five elements—metal, water, wood, fire, and earth—in order to create harmony and balance within all things. (Acupuncture and feng shui both draw from Taoist principles.)

Shintoism, Mugyo, Chinese folk religion, and Vietnamese folk religion focus on the aliveness of nature and the enduring consciousness of ancestors and cultural heroes.

Australia

The Aboriginal religion honors dreams, totem animals, ancestors, and the alive interconnectedness of everything. Its seemingly miraculous holistic healing practices draw upon a profound reverence for nature and the environment.

Europe

Ancient Celtic spirituality focused on the aliveness and interconnectedness of nature and the transcendence that underlies and illuminates the mundane. It possessed a complex pantheon of deities who could be invoked for various forms of support. (Some of these deities are still invoked by modern pagans today.) Stonehenge and structures like Stonehenge—precisely positioned in alignment with the position of the sun at solstices and equinoxes—illustrate the importance these ancient cultures attributed to the sun and the wheel of the year.

Ancient Germanic spirituality also featured a pantheon of gods and goddesses, each with their own unique magical attributes and myths.

Ancient Slavic spirituality was characterized by a deep respect for nature and the spirits that populated things like rivers, forests, and lakes.

North America

The spiritual systems of Native American tribes such as the Cherokee and Lakota share a reverence for nature and the elements. They draw upon the metaphysical properties of the natural world, acknowledging the sacredness of things like animals, plants, rocks, the sun, the moon, and the wind.

South America

The Inca, Aztecs, and Maya watched the stars and honored divinities aligned with the sun, moon, earth, and weather patterns. Like the ancient Egyptians and the Celts, they possessed highly evolved technologies that allowed them to build megalithic structures on a scope that continues to baffle modern science.

Reclaiming Our Heritage

The modern draw to magic, then—to a holistic and shamanic worldview—is natural. It is the instinct to reclaim who we are, what we know, and what we can do. At this point in our history, activities such as honoring the earth, marveling at the cosmos, and cooperating with our fellow humans are of more dire importance than financially or militarily defeating other countries or destroying the earth's resources for the sake of profit. Indeed, as so many of us know not just intellectually but also at a gut level, a cooperative relationship with the earth—as well as between genders, perspectives, races, and nationalities—will bring great blessings to our species.

························ YOUR MAGIC ·······················
Weave the Ancient Threads
Begin to weave and God will send the thread.
~ GERMAN PROVERB

You—your DNA blueprint, your consciousness, and even the components of your physical body—are woven from extremely ancient threads. This exercise will help you uncover and awaken the primordial power that is within you.

Sit someplace where you won't be disturbed. Light a violet- or lilac-colored pillar candle (this is the color of divine communion). Grab your notebook and a pen, and write down all you know about your heritage. What do you know about where your ancestors came from and what ancient spiritualities they may have practiced? If you're not sure, give it your best guess.

Next, list the ancient spiritualities and cultures you've been most drawn to and fascinated by in this lifetime. This list may coincide with your heritage, but it need not have anything to do with your DNA in this particular incarnation.

Now poke around on the web or visit a bookstore or library, and follow what feels most interesting and exciting to you to find one divine being or spiritual symbol from either of your two lists that really speaks to you. Obtain a representation of this being or symbol: paint it, draw it, print it out and frame it, or purchase a statue of any size depicting it. Place this representation next to the pillar candle in a special place to create a simple altar, a focal point for your magical spirituality. Relight the candle at intervals as an offering and a way of connecting with the Mystery and your spiritual inspiration.

3

Understanding the Dynamics

While it's certainly a spiritual path, magic is also a *craft*. Like other crafts, it can be a hobby or a calling, depending on your degree of commitment and enthusiasm. (Or it can start out as one and become the other. No value judgment here: both are fine.) Also like other crafts, it's a way of working with raw materials in order to bring your inner vision into physical reality.

But how does this work, exactly? What are the materials, and how can you use them to create the conditions you want to experience?

First and foremost, the material with which we craft is energy: specifically, the energy of everything, in all directions of time, as channeled through our physical being and shaped with our present-moment thoughts, intentions, visions, feelings, and expectations. As described in chapter 1, you're able to draw upon this energy because of your innate interconnection with the Great Holy Mystery, also known as eternity, infinity, and God/Goddess/All That Is. Then you're able to shape, steer, and set specific energetic conditions in motion through your personal present-moment perspective: your tiny, temporary human boat in the endless sea of existence.

In this book we'll be using words like *energy*, *vibration*, and *frequency* to describe the invisible material with which you will be crafting your magic. But spiritual and holistic healing traditions around the world have their own unique names for this energy. For example, Taoist traditions (like acupuncture and feng shui) call it *chi*. Reiki healers and other practitioners of Japanese healing arts call it *ki*. Yogis, Vedic astrologers, and Ayurvedic doctors call it *prana* and *akasha*. Ancient Egyptians called it *heka* or *ka*.

In chapter 6 we'll get into the specifics of energy work. For now we'll just be focusing on what this energy is and how it works.

Source Energy

The ancient text called the *Tao Te Ching* (as translated by Stephen Mitchell) states in chapter 6:

The Tao is called the Great Mother:
empty yet inexhaustible,
it gives birth to infinite worlds.

It is always present within you.
You can use it any way you want.

You might say that Lao-tzu, the author of the Tao Te Ching, which was written over a thousand years ago, was describing the unified theory that modern-day quantum physicists seek and what Albert Einstein may have meant when he said, "I want to know His [God's] thoughts; the rest are details." Similarly, scientific philosopher Ervin László, in the introduction to his seminal work *Science and the Akashic Field*, writes that "at the roots of reality there is not just matter and energy, but also a more subtle but equally fundamental factor, one that we can best describe as active and effective information.... [This information] links all things in the universe, atoms as well as galaxies, organisms the same as minds."

The Polarities

The classic magical text known as *The Kybalion* states in chapter 13, "Gender is in everything; everything has its Masculine and Feminine Principles; Gender manifests on all planes."

All is one at the core, and it manifests in the world as divine feminine and masculine polarities: the yin and yang. In the Hindu religion, this is the cosmic dance of Shiva and Shakti. Shiva is the divine masculine, the cosmos, and the unmanifest potential energy, while Shakti is the divine feminine, the earth, and all that we perceive through our senses. In Chinese cosmology, yin and yang represent not just feminine and masculine but also every other conceivable polarity: cold and hot, dark and light, small and large, quiet and loud, soft and hard, and so on.

Of course, the words *masculine* and *feminine* bring to mind our physical gender. Certainly, a fertile male and a fertile female can pool their respective genetic resources to create a new life with their polarized reproductive organs. And this is powerful magic indeed! But these energies—and what they create—work on a much subtler level as well. We each contain masculine and feminine energy within us, and when we become aware of the interplay of these qualities, we can balance them according to what will be most beneficial and harmonious for us, and utilize their co-creative abilities to magically bring forth the qualities and conditions we desire. (We will talk about how to do this in the next chapter. For now, I just want to introduce the concept.)

In countless cultures, we see the archetypal feminine and masculine represented in divine form. In addition to the examples just mentioned, Christianity gives us Jesus and the two Marys. Mother Mary and Mary Magdalene are two archetypal faces of the feminine principle: divine mother and divine lover. Buddhism gives us the Buddha in all his many forms and incarnations, but also Quan Yin and the many incarnations of Tara. Most polytheistic religions have numerous representations of both divine polarities. For example, the Greek pantheon alone gives us Rhea and Cronos, Zeus and Hera, Zeus and Demeter, Persephone and Hades, Aphrodite and Hephaestus, Aphrodite and Adonis, and Artemis and Apollo, to name just a few.

In certain Wiccan traditions, the divine masculine and divine feminine are often simply referred to as "the Lord and Lady." The Lord—the active principle—is associated with the sun and heavens, and the Lady—the receptive principle—is associated with the moon and the earth. We see these polarized divinities symbolically living out their lives through the cycles and seasons of the year. The Winter Solstice (as the time when the sun is reborn and the daylight hours begin to expand) is the birth of the masculine. Throughout the spring, as the days continue to get warmer and brighter, the God grows to manhood and falls in love with the Goddess. The summer is the full flowering of their romance. In the fall, as the darkness makes its slow return, the God then dwindles and dies before the divine masculine is reborn once again at the next Winter Solstice. (We'll go more deeply into the cycle of ancient holidays—also known as the wheel of the year—in chapter 5.)

The Elements

In chapter 3 of her book *The Western Guide to Feng Shui*, Terah Kathryn Collins writes, "Born out of the polaric interplay of yin and yang, the five elements manifest in countless ways and combinations around us."

Just as white light divides into the three primary colors, which in turn go on to combine and create the infinite gradations of color of a rainbow's rays, so do the polarities of the singular source energy give birth to the elements, which go on to give birth to everything in the seemingly finite world of form.

In many ancient healing and spiritual traditions, magical and shamanic practitioners perceive source energy as appearing in five elemental energies, the building blocks of all that we see and experience. In Western traditions, these are often earth, air, fire, water, and spirit. In India, they're earth, air, fire, water, and ether. In China, they're earth, wood, fire, water, and metal. While there are unmistakable parallels between the elemental traditions, there is also a uniquely beneficial wisdom associated with each.

In chapter 1 of *Science and the Akashic Field*, Ervin László writes, "According to the ancient cosmologies the universe's undifferentiated, all-encompassing consciousness separates off from its primordial unity and becomes localized in particular structures of matter."

With all of this in mind, the symbolism of a pentacle begins to come into focus.

The masculine principle can be thought of as the structure or the empty container in which all arises. The feminine principle can be thought of as that which arises: the manifested world of form. Underlying and interweaving both is source energy: the one, undifferentiated divine presence. These conditions give birth to the five elements.

Elemental wisdom is a way of perceiving energy at work in matter but also in thoughts, feelings, activities, and even subtler qualities. Once we learn to perceive the elements at work within all things, it makes sense to honor them as primal, conscious forces. We can also learn to invoke and collaborate with them in order to change the qualities of the energy that makes up the conditions of our lives, and thereby change our lives. (Again, for now I'm just introducing the conceptual framework of the elements. In the next chapter you'll find practical instructions for how to put this knowledge to use.)

Physical Materials

As you must have seen in movies and read about in books, many spells involve physical ingredients and tools: rocks, herbs, wands, brooms, sachets, cauldrons, candles, and such.

When I first got started on my magical path, I was unsure about the source of the effectiveness of the physical tools with which I worked. While I could sense that what I was doing was powerful, I found myself wondering things like "How exactly does this sprig of rosemary contribute to the success of my spell?" and "Does this candle have magical power on its own, or does it have something to do with being employed in this ritual?"

To shed light on the answers to questions like these, I'd like you to consider two outfits. The first is an outfit that you just never feel very attractive in. No matter what, when you wear it, your self-worth just isn't up to snuff. The second is an outfit that you always feel very attractive in. When you put it on, your eyes sparkle and you feel like the world is your oyster.

Now consider the vast difference each outfit can make in the outcomes of pivotal moments in your life, things like job interviews, dates, and chance encounters. Each can have a powerful hand in crafting an entirely different life story.

But is it really the outfit that has all this power? Well, yes … but also no. The power ultimately lies with *you*, doesn't it? The power is in how the outfit makes *you* look and feel, and therefore how *you* interact with the world and how the world interacts with you. So clearly, you can say that things are just things, but when those things are experienced by you, they can mean all the difference between living a spectacular life and living a life that leaves something to be desired.

So what is it about that fabulous outfit that makes you feel so good? Is it the color, the cut, the fabric? Is it the story of where you got it, or when you first wore it, or how you felt at those moments? The answer is it's all of those things, and something more. It's the miracle of the outfit's existence in space and time, as well as all of your associations with it. It's the transcendent being-ness of the outfit.

In other words, it's the outfit's *energy*.

So this isn't actually a metaphor for how magical tools and spell ingredients work; it's a literal description of it. If the outfit has so much power—not just to make you feel amazing the moment you put it on, but also to open doors of extravagant possibility—it's magic. *Everything* is magic, after all: everything is energy. Magic is the practice of becoming conscious of energy so that we can employ it to inspire us, uplift us, heal us, and craft conditions according to our will.

Magical Ethics

As the ubiquitous saying goes, "With great power comes great responsibility." When it comes to magical power, the main rule for being responsible is, conveniently, the same as the main rule for being effective: align with the Divine (the conscious, divine presence and the true oneness of All That Is) to shape conditions according to your highest and truest good, as well as the highest and truest good of all.

The only reason you would want to shape conditions in any other way would be because you were caught up in your ego. We all have an ego, of course, which I define as the illusion that we are disconnected: from other people, the planet, and All That Is. To put this another way, the only reason you would want to use magic to go against what is for the highest and truest good of all concerned would be because you were so convinced of your own separation and smallness. In truth, you're one with everything and everyone. It follows that your highest and truest good can't possibly be separate from the highest and truest good of everyone else.

This doesn't mean that you can't work magic for more money, or a better job, or to meet the love of your life. What it *does* mean is that you will benefit from learning the difference between an ego desire and an authentic desire. The following lists can help.

Ego Desires

- The desire to change other people's life experience
- The desire to have power over others
- The desire to attract a certain person
- The desire to get a specific job
- The desire to receive the income that would otherwise go to someone else
- The desire to prove to others how powerful you are

Authentic Desires

- The desire to change your own life experience (including the way you experience others)
- The desire to embody your natural authority, or to remove the power other people have over you

- The desire to attract a partner who is perfect for you
- The desire to get a job that is perfect for you in every way
- The desire to receive your own abundant income
- The desire to embody your natural power

You'll notice that authentic desires place fewer limitations on the outcome. As such, manifesting authentic desires allows room for the universe (the Mystery and the source of all magical power) to flow in. The ego likes to assume it knows what's best, when in reality it can't possibly do so, because it can't see the whole picture. The part of us that is one with everything, on the other hand, can see it all, and create doors of amazing opportunity of which our ego (our separate self) couldn't have begun to conceive. Clearly, ethical magic is best for everyone.

In fact, I often wonder if some of the fear around magical work is created because so many beginners cast their first spells based on ego desires rather than authentic ones. The magical mess such an action can create can't be overstated, because energetically, *what we send out always comes back to us multiplied.* For example:

- A love spell on a specific person can set in motion an abusive relationship that ends up enslaving you right along with the other person (because you overrode the other person's free will).
- A spell to bump someone out of a job so you can have it can set up an eventual money drain (because you worked magic based on the premise that there's not enough to go around).
- A spell to have power over someone can eventually cause you to feel completely trapped, stuck, and depressed (because you sent out the energy of oppression).

On the other hand, when your entire spiritual path—which includes your magical work—is geared toward connecting with, marveling at, and co-creating with the divine presence (the Great Mystery, God/Goddess, All That Is), everything you do ultimately increases your positive momentum and attunes your life experience to greater levels of health, happiness, and abundance. (If, knowing all of this, you still can't seem to dissuade yourself from wanting to do a spell that infringes on someone else's free will, consider this a valuable diagnostic tool identifying a deep-seated psychological issue. In such a case, it would be a good idea to put your magical studies on hold and seek quality counseling.)

········· YOUR MAGIC ·········

Pick Up on Crystal Energy

Crystals are the blossoms of the mineralogical portion of the Earth; the recognition of the beauty and loving energies of these forms can greatly enhance one's personal development. They are the myriad fireworks of both creativity and individual universal energies.

~ MELODY, *LOVE IS IN THE EARTH*

A lot of us fall in love with crystals early on in our magical path. This is perhaps because we find working with them to be one of the easiest and most immediate ways to connect with the unseen aliveness and energy in the natural world.

For this exercise, simply locate and then visit a metaphysical bookstore, rock shop, jewelry boutique, or craft fair in your area. Basically any vendor that carries gemstones that you are allowed to spend time with and touch will do. It's best if you do this alone so that you can really relax and get into the zone.

Once you arrive, begin to breathe consciously. Relax and come into the present moment as best you can. (There is no need to close your eyes, hyperventilate, or do anything that will draw unwanted attention.) When you feel ready to connect with the energy of the crystals, begin by just being present with their beauty. Which ones catch your eye and call to you the most? Let your intuition lead you to the ones you'd like to pick up and hold. When you hold them, relax and see if you can feel any particular energetic qualities: any emotions, inner guidance, or physical sensations. Don't be discouraged if you don't notice anything in particular. Know that even if you just like some crystals better than others—perhaps because of their color, weight, or texture—that's still a way of connecting with their energy. (Remember the outfit example?)

Spend as much time with this investigation as feels valuable to you. There's no need to actually make a purchase, but there's also no harm in bringing one or more crystals home with you if you'd like. Just don't swipe anything! Doing so would indicate that you hold the belief that you don't have enough money for all the things you want, and taking action on such a belief will be sure to set up a financial challenge for you in the future—and that would be an unfortunate misuse of your magical power. Instead, keep reading this book and learn how to attract plenty of money for everything you want and need. Then come back and get your crystals later.

The purpose of this exercise is to help you realize how connected to energy you already are. The more you continue to engage in exercises like this one, the more aware of energy you will become over time.

4

Connecting with Power

Look at you! You've already learned so much.

Now let's get more specific and explore the building blocks of practical magic. This chapter will get you acquainted with each of the five elements, give you a working understanding of divine energies and archetypes, and coach you in discovering a personal, present-moment cosmology that connects you to your power.

Earth

Earth is a good, solid place to start. You could say that every tangible thing in the physical world falls in this category, although if it isn't dirt, a rock, or the actual ground, it has other elemental properties mixed in. For example, doves are very much aligned with the air element, lions with the fire element, and salmon with the water element. Similarly, while flowers, herbs, and crystals inarguably fall in the category of the earth element, various varieties have additional elemental associations. Cayenne pepper is a fiery herb, for example, and an aquamarine is a watery stone.

Spiritually, the earth element is connected with silence, stillness, physical nourishment, and a deep sense of grounded connectedness. Imagine a majestic forest at midnight or the subterranean stillness of a cave.

The cardinal direction associated with the earth element is north. When you face that direction fully and with consciousness, you can get a sense of earth's power.

Work with the earth element when you want to:

- Gain stillness

- Feel grounded

- Connect with your family, heritage, and traditions

- Heal your sexuality

- Attract prosperity

Symbols of the earth element that are appropriate for an altar or a ritual circle include:

- Crystals and minerals

- Plants

- Soil

- Ceramic dishes or plates (Traditionally, plates inscribed with a pentacle—a five-pointed star surrounded by a circle—are used for this purpose.)

Air

The air element fuels the winds of change, and then you dance on it when a wonderful new condition blows in. More literally, it's what you're drawing in and out of your lungs at this very moment. It's also wind, clouds, and the sky. Winged creatures are aligned with the air element, as are crystals and plants with qualities of freshness, lightness, and buoyancy.

Spiritually, the air element is connected with knowledge, words, ideas, healing, and new beginnings. Imagine a sparkly clear sky at dawn or the song of wind chimes and a breeze blowing through leaves.

The cardinal direction associated with the air element is east. When you face that direction fully and with consciousness, you can get a sense of air's power.

Work with the air element when you want to:

• Gain clarity

• Feel refreshed

• Connect with knowledge through written or spoken language

• Heal your physical body

• Attract a positive new beginning

Symbols of the air element that are appropriate for an altar or a ritual circle include:

• Smoking incense (with a holder)

• Naturally shed feathers

• A fan

• A chime

• Bells

Fire

Fire sparks passion of all varieties. It appears in the world as lights, candles, sparkles, warmth, actual fire, and the sun. Reptiles, lions, tigers, and dragonflies are associated with the fire element, as are herbs with heat to them, such as cayenne, cinnamon, and ginger.

Spiritually, the fire element is associated with shining our light and sharing our gifts in an authentic way—a way that nourishes us and brings grace to the world. It ignites the inner flame that fuels our attraction, enthusiasm, action, and rage. Connect with it through the vision of a raging brushfire or the blazing sun above a desert landscape, high in the noonday sky.

The cardinal direction associated with the fire element is south. When you face that direction fully and with consciousness, you can get a sense of fire's power.

Work with the fire element when you want to:

- Spark action
- Activate success
- Ignite your fame or recognition
- Transmute negativity into positivity
- Express or inspire passion
- Shield yourself, your loved ones, or your home in protective, fiery light

Symbols of the fire element that are appropriate for an altar or a ritual circle include:

- Candles
- A light catcher or prism
- An oil burner (i.e., an aromatherapy diffuser with a tealight)

Water

A gentle, cleansing substance that is precious to all life, water can also cut through solid plains to make room for raging rivers and dissolve huge rocks into sand. Water-dwelling creatures of all varieties are aligned with the water element, as are many sweet-smelling blooms, such as roses, lilies, lilac, and jasmine.

Spiritually, the water element is associated with cleansing, healing, poetry, music, dreams, intuition, and the spirit world. It allows us to plumb our own depths in order to touch that part of us that is always inspired and in awe. In turn, this prevents burnout by infusing all that we do with inspiration and joy. Imagine gazing out at a vast ocean and watching the sunset while waist-deep in the waves.

The cardinal direction associated with the water element is west. When you face that direction fully and with consciousness, you can get a sense of water's power.

Work with the water element when you want to:

- Heal your emotions
- Remember your dreams
- Connect with your intuition
- Communicate with deceased loved ones
- Align with your authentic life path

Symbols of the water element that are appropriate for an altar or a ritual circle include:

- A chalice or bottle filled with water
- A water globe (like a snow globe, only reminiscent of the ocean)
- Seashells

Spirit

Remember how I said that dirt, rocks, and the ground are purely in the domain of the earth element? That's true in a sense, but in another sense it's not. Because everything—and I mean *everything*—is infused with the spirit element as well. In fact, ultimately, everything is *pure* spirit element temporarily masquerading as something else.

Of course, this element is no different from the unified field of energy before it split off into the masculine and feminine energies, the elements, and the entire manifest world. But because spirit is still so undeniably present within us and within all that we see and experience, we acknowledge it as one of the five elements as well.

On a personal level, we can connect with the spirit element by imagining our energy field like a tree trunk extending deep into the earth and high into the sky, connecting with the radiant light at the core of the earth and the shimmering energy of the cosmos. As children of the earth and the cosmos, this is actually our natural energetic state, which is why consciously conceiving of our energy as being connected in this way provides a natural, sustained, and balancing flow of energy. This is also why so many ancient cultures have some variation of the Tree of Life, which symbolically unites the earth, the cosmos, and the human experience.

Work with the spirit element when you want to:

• Connect more strongly with your power

• Feel simultaneously grounded and inspired

• Remember your true identity

• Channel healing and magical energy from the earth and the cosmos

Symbols of the spirit element that are appropriate for an altar or a ritual circle include:

• Sacred symbols, such as sigils, runes, and mandalas

• Three-dimensional sacred geometric shapes, such as merkaba quartz crystals and pyramids

• Wands made of crystal and / or wood

The Divine Feminine

You might think of the divine feminine as simply "the Goddess." She appears in an infinite number of forms and possesses countless emanations. Indeed, to many of us, and certainly through the lens of the polarities, every goddess of every tradition is a face of the *one* Goddess, as is every feminine person and the entire manifest world.

When conceptualizing the most primordial interplay of divine feminine and divine masculine energies, you might think of the masculine, the God, as emptiness, formlessness, and pure potentiality, and also as the container in which the divine feminine arises. Conversely, the Goddess is every manifested thing: everything that possesses form, color, texture, taste, aroma, or sound.

If the Goddess is a dancer, the God is the stage.

If the Goddess is a song, the God is the moments of silence between the notes.

If the Goddess is a firework, the God is the sky.

If the Goddess is life, the God is death.

If the Goddess is rage, the God is indifference.

If the Goddess is beauty, the God is the consciousness that perceives beauty.

If the Goddess is love, the God is freedom.

The tarot provides powerful examples of this polarity dynamic in the Emperor and Empress cards, as well as the Magician and Priestess cards. While the Emperor rules his world and expresses his reigning freedom by imposing a firm structure and strict discipline on his subjects, the Empress employs her position to provide love, gifting her subjects with nourishment, sustenance, and compassion. And while the Magician channels invisible energy in order to live the life he wants in accordance with his desire for freedom, the Priestess works with the tides, the moon cycles, and her own inner creative force in order to bring forth life and all visible things in accordance with her desire to love. In our inner landscape, it's easy to see how each archetype needs the other in order to thrive in all areas of life.

Here's a separate but complementary way of thinking of the dance of the polarities: The feminine principle is attractive and receptive. She stays in one place and draws things toward herself with her beauty and her light. The masculine principle is proactive and dynamic. He formulates plans and takes action with his single-pointed focus. (While this paradigm is different from the first one presented here, its principles are still mirrored in the tarot cards just mentioned.)

If the Goddess is the earth, the God is the thunderstorm that waters her.

If the Goddess is the moon, the God is the sun that illuminates her.

If the Goddess is a mermaid sitting on an island, singing and brushing her long hair, the God is the bold sailor who is drawn into her orbit by her beauty and her haunting song.

Still, the Goddess cannot be pigeonholed. While she is birth, youth, and beauty, she is also ferocity, old age, and death. And while she is the Great Mother of immense gentleness and compassion, she will also not hesitate to violently destroy anything that incites her rage. To steal a turn of phrase from Walt Whitman, the Goddess is vast: she contains multitudes. There is *one* constant, though, and that is love. No matter what other traits the Goddess may be expressing, at her core she is always love itself: the power that comprises the physical world and keeps it spinning.

Here's a sampling of the Goddess's many faces and archetypes:

- The Goddess appears as **a priestess of creativity and magic**: for example, as the Egyptian goddess Isis, the Celtic goddess Brighid, the Hindu goddess Saraswati, and the orisha Yemaya. In this form, she helps us create all forms of art and masterfully work with energy in order to heal ourselves and others and effect all forms of positive change according to our will.

- She appears as **a dark matron of rage and/or death**: for example, as the Hindu goddess Kali, the Greek goddess Hecate, the Hawaiian goddess Pele, the Norse goddess Hel, and the Celtic goddess the Morrigan. In this form, she helps us release ego attachments, connect with hidden wisdom, and take dynamic action to heal conditions of unfairness and oppression.

- She appears as **a great mother of compassion and nourishment**: for example, as the Christian figure Mary, the Greek goddess Demeter, the Buddhist divinity Quan Yin, and the Egyptian goddess Hathor. In this form, she helps us feel loved and lovable, heal our hearts, and connect with the innate healing wisdom of our physical bodies.

- She appears as **the quintessence of beauty, luxury, and love**: for example, as the Greek goddess Aphrodite, the Hindu goddesses Lakshmi and Radha, and the Yoruban orisha Oshun. In this form, she helps us emanate our natural radiance, open up to receiving wealth, and experience satisfying romance.

- She appears **as a paragon of fierceness and strength**: for example, as the Norse goddess Freya, the Hindu goddess Durga, the Greek goddess Artemis, and the Egyptian goddess Sekhmet. In this form, she helps us own our power, speak our truth, and achieve success.

- She appears as **a being of great wisdom and adaptability**: for example, as the Greek goddesses Athena and Persephone, the Egyptian goddess Bast, and the Buddhist goddess Tara. In this form, she helps us perceive the underlying dynamics of situations and conditions, illuminate ideal solutions, and frame our life experiences in empowering ways.

By invoking these various aspects of the Goddess, we can invoke those aspects within ourselves, and thus awaken or intensify our own inherent power, wisdom, and joy.

The Divine Masculine

You may like to think of the divine masculine presence as simply "the God." Although if you *don't* like to, I don't blame you one bit. The word *God* (with a capital G) has accumulated some pretty serious baggage in the more recent chapters of human history. But when the polarized creative forces come together—the Goddess *and* the God—each plays an equally important role in the creation and maintenance of all that we see and are. In a way, everything is birthed from their union. In her book *Awakening Shakti*, Sally Kempton says: "In the Indian view of creation, Desire—Kama—is always the first seed of life. … Cosmic desire brings the universe into being, and the world is, in one sense, an outflowing of the cosmic erotic impulse."

Of course, at his core, the God is the primordial masculine force. And, like the Goddess, he also manifests in a number of ways. Here's a sampling:

- The God appears as **a paragon of untamable wildness**: for example, as the Greek gods Pan and Dionysus, the Celtic god Cernunnos, and the Norse god Loki. In this form, he helps us tap into our wildness and sexual freedom, and shifts our everyday reality in unexpected (and possibly very empowering) ways.

- He appears as **a magician of great wisdom and power:** for example, as the Celtic divinity and cultural hero Merlin, the Greek god Hermes, the Egyptian god Thoth, and the Norse god Odin. In this form, he helps us learn how to shape and manipulate the inner and outer dynamics of life to create positive change according to our will.

- He appears as **a proactive, obstacle-demolishing force**: for example, as the Hindu god Ganesh, the Egyptian god Osiris, the Norse god Forseti, and the Christian divinity John the Baptist. In this form, he helps us find swift justice, bust through blocks, and clear the way for blessings to flow.

- He appears as **a contemplative and meditative prophet**: for example, as Buddha, Jesus, Mohammed, and the Christian mystic Saint Francis of Assisi. In this form, he helps us connect with the formless and eternal—that which is beyond the physical and outside of the ego.

- He appears as **a radiant warrior:** for example, as the Greek god Ares, the Celtic god Lugh, and the Hindu god Kartikeya. In this form, he helps us rise to challenges and achieve glorious success.

• He appears as **a majestic ruler and king**: for example, as the Aztec god Quetzalcoatl, the Celtic god the Dagda, the Hindu god Vishnu, and the Greek god Zeus. In this form, he helps us build the strong foundations and habits that allow us to reach our goals and master our lives.

Just like with the Goddess, invoking various incarnations of the divine masculine will allow you to activate their attributes within your own psyche for the purpose of creating positive change in your life experience.

The Divine Presence

At the heart of it all, all goddesses are one Goddess, just as all gods are one God. Even more fundamentally, the one God and one Goddess (and everything else in the seen and unseen worlds) are one presence: the All, the Great Mystery, or, simply, the Divine.

To describe the divine presence, let's revisit the Tao Te Ching (chapter 25), as translated by Stephen Mitchell:

There was something formless and perfect
before the universe was born.
It is serene. Empty.
Solitary. Unchanging.
Infinite. Eternally present. ...

It flows through all things,
inside and outside, and returns
to the origin of all things.

Let's also look at this quote by Carl Sagan in his book *Cosmos*:

The cosmos is also within us. We're made of star-stuff. We are a way for the cosmos to know itself.

In your magical work, you may at times (or even at all times) feel drawn to invoke this singular divine presence, rather than the divine feminine, the divine masculine, or a particular deity. When you do so, you are connecting with all power, all knowledge, and all wisdom. This is a way of transcending the illusion of you—the temporary human form and limited human brain—and connecting with who you really are: Infinity. The cosmos. The origin of all things. The universe, getting to know itself.

Your Personal Cosmology

At any given time, there is a cosmological prism through which divine light shines in a way that will inspire you deeply. It could be a particular cultural pantheon and accompanying set of spiritual myths. It could be wildflowers in your region, and the secrets they whisper as they quiver in the breeze. It could be the glittering night sky and the sacred geometric dance of the planets. It could be the songs of the Beatles or the films of David Lynch. Or it could be all of these things, at various times. Almost certainly, it is a mash-up: an inspirational patchwork quilt that is unique to you.

There is a popular chant about the Goddess that was written by the author Starhawk. It goes, "She changes everything she touches, and everything she touches changes." Indeed, it is accurate to describe this human experience as constant change: an unending surrender to the transformational cauldron of the Goddess.

That's why I subscribe to the belief that a healthy, vibrant relationship to the realm of the Divine is constantly in flux. Today you might be working with Quan Yin to heal old sexual wounds with compassion. And when those wounds are healed, she may float away on her lotus and reappear on the seashore of your consciousness as Aphrodite, to help you own your sexuality with radiant self-assurance.

There may be constants throughout your life. Perhaps you always like to work with the Greek pantheon, or you never fail to find deep inspiration by looking at the stars. Or you might completely reinvent your spirituality every few years.

As we've seen, there is ultimately one consciousness at the heart of everything. So no matter how the view through your spiritual kaleidoscope may appear to change throughout your life, it's always the same kaleidoscope. At its core, it's always the divine presence, the cosmos, the Great Holy Mystery. So the question is always: What inspires me today? What allows me to connect with who and what I really am: eternal, infinite, powerful, and divine?

· YOUR MAGIC ·

Create a Proper Altar

The creation of an altar is a sacred act, an act of power and grace.
~ DENISE LINN, *ALTARS*

Remember your simple candle altar from the exercise in chapter 2? In this exercise you're going to expand on it (or change it altogether) so that you have a proper altar for your magic and ritual work. If it's not already on a surface that feels right to you for a slightly more elaborate altar, find or obtain a surface that is. It can be something as simple as an end table or nightstand. It's ideal if it's placed in an area where you can sit in front of it to meditate or do ritual work without being disturbed.

If it feels right, you might like to spread a cloth over your altar surface. Visit a fabric store or a shop with a good selection of tapestries or scarves to find the fabric that feels exactly right.

Choose a focal object for your altar. This could be the image you chose in chapter 2, or it could be something else entirely. It could be a symbol or framed picture or statue of a divinity, a pair of divinities (such as a particular goddess and god), or a group of divinities (such as angels). But it could also be something unconventional, like a framed postcard of a forest or a picture of the earth from space. The important thing is to choose whatever best anchors your sense of expansive connection to your power and the realm of the Divine.

Next, select a symbol for each of the five elements. (Revisit the elements material at the beginning of this chapter for ideas.) Then take some time to arrange them around your altar focal object in a way that feels right to you.

Finally, place one or more offerings on your altar: gifts of love from you to the Divine. Popular offerings include fruit, flowers, crystals, bowls of dried herbs, shiny coins, and treats that won't attract ants, such as coffee beans, unopened bottles of beer, or wrapped candy. When choosing your offering(s), you may want to consider the focal object you've chosen and what that particular divinity or symbol might prefer.

Now you have a visual representation of your magical consciousness and a uniquely sacred space where your awareness of form meets and merges with your awareness of spirit. By offering physical items to the spiritual forces, you have opened a doorway to the spirit realm. Keep it alive and open by tending to your altar. Keep your offerings fresh, burn candles and incense on the altar, and fine-tune the altar's appearance according to what inspires you each day.

5

Aligning with Time

Albert Einstein once wrote in a letter, "The distinction between past, present, and future is only a stubbornly persistent illusion." Indeed, from our human perspective, it appears that we are in a constant dance to the music of time. When we work magic, we work within this appearance to create positive change according to our will. As such, a considerable aspect of owning your power involves moving harmoniously with the flow of time: attuning to the energies at play at various moments and using them to fuel your magical work.

A worker of magic seeks to be a masterful captain of a ship on the sea of time, watching the sky, the water, and the wind in order to safely steer to her destination while enjoying every second of the ride.

Naturally, you can enhance the effectiveness of your spells and rituals by choosing an auspicious time to perform them, and the information in this chapter will show you how to do that. But first, it's important to simply become aware of the time-related energies that predominate in any given moment, and to begin to sensitize yourself to their frequencies.

The Phases of the Moon

If time is like a drumbeat, then the phases of the moon are like a melody: a repetitive, mellifluous sequence of notes that cyclically rise and fall. To get in the habit of being aware of the current moon phase (as well as other aspects mentioned in this chapter), I highly recommend getting an almanac that provides each day's moon phase and sign. *Llewellyn's Magical Almanac* and *Llewellyn's Witches' Calendar* are good choices, or you can also find comprehensive moon information online, for example on the site lunarium.co.uk.

The basic energies associated with each phase of the moon are as follows:

- **The new moon** is the dawn of a fresh new cycle. It's perfect for setting new intentions and beginning new projects. It's an appropriate time to work magic for fresh beginnings and the expansion of new conditions.

- **The waxing moon** is a time when energy is expanding and momentum is building. It's a time for magic related to increasing and attracting desired conditions.

- **The full moon** holds great power because the lunar cycle has reached its climax. Any magic performed during this time will be supercharged with heightened energy. It's perfect for magic related to blessing, empowering, and summoning conditions you desire.

- **The waning moon** lends the power to banish, reduce, diminish, and cleanse. The lunar cycle's energy is dissipating and unwinding, so it's powerful for magic related to letting go of conditions you no longer desire.

- **The dark moon** (the day before the new moon) is the silence between the notes, or the moment after your exhale but before your inhale. It's a time of profound stillness and rest. Its energies can be channeled toward deep inner work, healing, cleansing, and releasing.

Astrology

Much like magic itself, you could study astrology for a lifetime and still leave plenty left unlearned. Whether or not you feel drawn to go deep into your astrological studies, you'll find it helpful to have a basic understanding of certain key aspects, namely, the sun sign and the moon sign of any given day. Knowing these two signs will give you an idea of the broadest strokes of energy at work. In addition to helping you plan your spells, this information will help you understand and predict the moods and motivations of other people and yourself.

As you're likely aware, there are twelve signs of the zodiac, and the sun moves into each of these for a roughly equal length of time each year. This is what the layperson generally thinks of when they think of astrology. In response to the classic conversation starter "What's your sign?" we generally answer with the sign the sun was in on the day we were born. Because the sun is so prominent (in the sky and in one's astrology chart), this sign can give you powerful insight into a person's character: their values, tendencies, and reasons for doing what they do. Similarly, the sun sign of any given moment influences everyone. In other words, while people born under the sun sign of Aries are known for being impulsive and outgoing, *everyone* will feel just a bit more impulsive and outgoing when the sun is in Aries.

Many people are not aware that the moon—which changes signs every two to three days—also plays a significant role in the personality. While the sun influences the most obvious, outwardly shining aspects of our character, the moon presides over the inner realm: our more private thoughts, feelings, and emotions. (If you don't already know your moon sign, if you know the time you were born, you can discover your moon sign for free online at sites such as www.alabe.com/freechart.) Regardless of when you were born, the current moon sign influences you. While the sun influences the overarching energies at work, the moon—being much closer to the earth than the sun—has a more personal, present-moment effect, as it moves more rapidly from sign to sign.

You'll find that knowing what signs the sun and moon are in, and understanding the dynamics of each sign, does a lot more than support your magical and intuitive efforts. Each sign has its strengths, and consciously tapping into these strengths is a natural way of keeping your life in well-rounded harmony.

It's also helpful to be aware of the qualities that show up when the energies related to each sign are being blocked or not being harmoniously expressed. For example, Leos typically are naturally outgoing and enjoy being in the spotlight, but when they judge these qualities in themselves, they can appear to be introverted and shy. In turn, this fosters frustration and loneliness, because they are not connecting with others in a way that expresses their true nature. Similarly, when the moon is in Capricorn, we often naturally feel like accomplishing things and marking things off our to-do list. But if you're fighting this desire because it's the weekend, you may become irritated and grumpy. Once you understand this dynamic, you can make a decision that supports your harmony by working with the prevailing energies, such as choosing to spend the day cleaning the garage rather than going for a leisurely walk in the park.

There are plenty of books and websites that will allow you to delve much more deeply into the study of each sign. But here is a general introduction to each of the twelve signs, as well as the unique energies they share when visited by the sun and moon. For everyday purposes (i.e., planning spells and tapping into the unique energy of the day), the following descriptions will be sufficient. At any rate, they're a fine place to start.

Aries

Aries is a fire sign, ruled by the planet Mars and symbolically represented as the ram. Starting on the first day of spring, Aries loves starting things and has a youthful exuberance. While its shadow side is impatience, this same aspect can be channeled toward getting stuck energy moving again and propelling ourselves out of ruts.

- When the sun is in Aries, write out your goals, meet new people, and try new things.
- When the moon is in Aries, work magic and take actions related to setting new intentions, manifesting new conditions, and getting stuck energy moving.
- Blocked Aries energy can manifest as restlessness or depression. Even if you don't want to, you'll probably feel better if you get out or start something new.

Taurus

Taurus is an earth sign, ruled by the planet Venus and symbolically represented as the bull. Taurus has a sturdy, steadfast vibration, and also loves the sensual, earthly realm. While its shadow side is stubbornness, this same aspect can be channeled toward sticking to our commitments, values, and goals.

- When the sun is in Taurus, take concrete steps toward manifesting your goals and desired long-term conditions, and focus on physical self-care (exercise, healthy eating, grooming, etc.).

- When the moon is in Taurus, work magic and take actions related to permanence, commitment, physical health, and sensual enjoyment.

- Blocked Taurus energy can manifest as boredom. If you're experiencing this when the sun or moon is in Taurus, ask yourself what you really want in life, and what action steps will help you establish these conditions. Go deep: don't discount the things you want just because they require a lot of work.

Gemini

Gemini is an air sign, ruled by the planet Mercury and symbolically represented by the twins. Gemini is sparkling, rapidly moving, charismatic, and idea-filled. While its shadow side is extreme changeability (like Dr. Jekyll and Mr. Hyde), this same aspect can be channeled toward maintaining an open mind and a flexible perspective.

- When the sun is in Gemini, study the things that interest you, write in your journal, and do things differently than you usually do, just for fun.

- When the moon is in Gemini, work magic and take actions related to gaining clarity, communicating effectively, and shifting your vibration.

- Blocked Gemini energy can show up as inertia: a feeling of being stuck. It's very likely that reading or studying something that interests you will reawaken you to the magic of life.

Cancer

Cancer is a water sign, ruled by the moon and symbolically represented by the crab. Cancer is devoted, nurturing, and deeply sensitive. After all, crabs have a hard outer shell only because they're so soft on the inside. While Cancer's shadow side is possessiveness, this same aspect can be channeled toward creating stability and loyally maintaining lifelong relationships.

- When the sun is in Cancer, beautify your home environment, nurture yourself, and spend time with family and friends.

- When the moon is in Cancer, work magic and take actions related to loving yourself, supporting others, and creating a harmonious home.

- Blocked Cancer energy can show up as a tender, unexplained emotional ache in the heart area, or as feeling shut off from your heart completely. To remedy either condition, try reaching out to someone you love or cuddling with a partner or pet.

Leo

Leo is a fire sign, ruled by the sun and symbolically represented by the lion. Leo is a natural leader and loves socializing, being seen, and being in the spotlight. While its shadow side is self-centeredness, this same aspect can be channeled toward leading and inspiring others by example.

- When the sun is in Leo, plan parties, attend social gatherings, and share your gifts with others.
- When the moon is in Leo, work magic and take actions related to sharing your gifts, shining your light, owning your confidence, and excelling in leadership roles.
- As already mentioned, blocked Leo energy can manifest as introversion, frustration, and loneliness. You can move through these by asking yourself what you would most like to be known for in your heart of hearts. What gifts would you like to share? How would you like to be seen? Then take steps to bravely share these aspects of yourself with the world.

Virgo

Virgo is an earth sign, ruled by Mercury and symbolically represented by an independent woman. (To the ancients, the word *virgin* didn't necessarily mean what it means to us today. Rather, it described a woman who may like men but doesn't need a man.) Virgo is meticulous: it keeps an eye on details and enjoys creating order and harmony in the inner and outer realms. While its shadow side might be described as nitpicky, this same aspect can be channeled toward helping heal and release patterns that no longer serve, thereby creating greater beauty, health, and harmony on all levels.

- When the sun is in Virgo, take systematic steps to create order in your mind, body, spirit, and home.

- When the moon is in Virgo, work magic and take actions related to cleansing, clearing, organizing, and bolstering physical health.

- Blocked Virgo energy can show up as intense messiness and/or disorganization. This happens when we are so focused on the details that we feel overwhelmed. Then, instead of dealing with all of them, we completely give up. If you're experiencing blocked Virgo energy, clear clutter from your home. Don't think about all of it: just thoroughly clear out one limited area, such as the medicine cabinet. Repeat as needed.

Libra

Libra is an air sign, ruled by Venus and symbolically represented by balancing scales. Libra loves fairness, aesthetic beauty, and balance of all varieties. While its shadow side is frivolity, this same aspect can be channeled toward keeping things light while deeply appreciating art and the beauty of the physical world.

- When the sun is in Libra, establish a healthy equilibrium in your life between work and play, effort and relaxation.

- When the moon is in Libra, work magic and take actions related to physical beauty, balance, harmony, art, and romance.

- Blocked Libra energy can show up as heaviness and negativity. Try shifting your focus from what you perceive to be ugly and wrong about life to all the beautiful blessings that surround you: the sky, the trees, your loved ones, music, and all forms of uplifting art.

Scorpio

Scorpio is a water sign, ruled by Pluto and symbolically represented by the scorpion. Scorpio is a complex and charismatic sign: it fearlessly delves into life's mysterious depths. While its shadow side is jealousy, this same aspect can be channeled toward abiding passion in intimate love.

- When the sun is in Scorpio, gaze fearlessly beyond the veil: make peace with death and connect with deceased loved ones on the other side.

- When the moon is in Scorpio, work magic and take actions related to sexuality, attraction, solving mysteries, and revealing secrets.

- Blocked Scorpio energy can manifest as sexual repression. Due to the nature of repression, you might not know that's what you're experiencing. Clues would be unexplained health issues (such as restless leg syndrome, headaches, or challenges with reproductive organs), sexual thoughts you keep hidden, addictions, a complete disconnection from or lack of identification with sexuality, or abusive behavior. If you think you might be experiencing a mild Scorpio block, take steps to experience your sexuality in a way that feels fun to you, alone or with a partner. Deeper and more longstanding Scorpio blocks will benefit from qualified counseling.

Sagittarius

Sagittarius is a fire sign, ruled by Jupiter and symbolically represented by the archer (a centaur with a bow and arrow). Sagittarius is lucky, expansive, adventurous, and gregarious. It finds great joy in traveling to exotic places and meeting all sorts of interesting people. While its shadow side is extravagance, this same aspect can be channeled toward all forms of generosity.

- When the sun is in Sagittarius, prioritize adventure of all kinds: plan trips and vacations, meet new people, learn new things, and take different routes to work.

- When the moon is in Sagittarius, work magic and take actions related to luck, success, expansion, travel, and fun.

- Blocked Sagittarius energy can manifest as binge-watching shows or excessively escaping into fantasy novels. While these things are great for relaxing sometimes, if they become a stand-in for your social life, try taking a trip somewhere fun and experiencing an adventure of your own.

Capricorn

Capricorn is an earth sign, ruled by Saturn and symbolically represented by the goat. Capricorn is independent, focused, disciplined, and exceptionally successful at reaching goals. While its shadow side could be called harshly critical, this same aspect can be channeled toward achieving and maintaining impeccable excellence.

- When the sun is in Capricorn, set goals and clearly outline the action steps you'll need to take in order to achieve them. Also use this time to break negative habits and establish positive ones.

- When the moon is in Capricorn, work magic and take actions related to setting and reaching goals, working hard, and establishing independence.

- Blocked Capricorn energy can appear as seeming laziness and procrastination. These may arise in response to a limiting belief that no matter how hard you work, you cannot actually achieve what you desire (so why bother?), or as some sort of rebellion against the innate desire to work toward the things you care about. In either case, you will benefit from journaling about what you'd really like to achieve in this lifetime and then taking a clear, honest look at how you might go about actually doing so.

Aquarius

Aquarius is an air sign, ruled by Uranus and symbolically represented by the water bearer (a person carrying a pitcher of water). Aquarius is wonderfully unique, with a singular ability to perceive things without looking through the lens of convention. This makes Aquarian insights both radical and invaluable. While its shadow side is self-aggrandizement, this same aspect can be channeled toward fearlessly being oneself and speaking one's truth.

- When the sun is in Aquarius, do things you wouldn't normally do and say things you wouldn't normally say. Throw off expectations and convention in order to get to know yourself better.

- When the moon is in Aquarius, work magic and take actions related to expressing creativity, speaking your truth, being yourself, and gaining a fresh perspective.

- Blocked Aquarius energy can appear as a fear of being perceived as different or weird. This will stifle your true self and can eventually lead to depression. So give up on trying to fit in, and instead revel in the things that make you unique. This will attract people who appreciate who you really are, rather than people who are intimidated by your inimitable form of fabulousness.

Pisces

Pisces is a water sign, ruled by Neptune and symbolically represented by two fish swimming in opposite directions. Pisces is the most watery of water signs, aligned with poetry, music, and the deepest, most dreamlike depths of the sea. While its shadow side could be described as spacing out or living in a dream world, this same aspect can be channeled toward creating immensely beautiful artwork and providing extremely useful intuitive information.

- When the sun is in Pisces, focus on sleeping deeply. Keep your bedroom restful and your bed comfortable. Exercise, go light on the caffeine, and keep a dream journal near your bed.
- When the moon is in Pisces, work magic and take actions related to intuition, creativity, and sleep.
- Blocked Pisces energy can manifest as stress. When we devalue the importance of sleep, dreams, and fantasies, we get out of balance and feel we have to force other aspects of life to work. We may find ourselves drinking too much caffeine or losing our usual inspiration. Come back into balance by prioritizing sleep and relaxation. Perhaps get a professional massage or take a warm bath by candlelight.

Times of Power

The day is a year in microcosm. Just as spring is a favorite time for romance, and fall is when we get excited about wearing scarves and having pumpkin-flavored everything, each time of the day has its own unique energetic qualities. Knowing these qualities allows us to align our magical workings with the times of day that will best empower our intentions.

Midnight is a portal. It's the precise moment when we stop descending into the darkness of one day and start ascending toward the light of the next. This makes it a time of great power. It infuses our magic with transformational energy. It helps us to banish what doesn't serve as one day falls away and to birth what we desire as one day begins anew.

Sunrise is also a portal. (You'll find that portals of all varieties are highly valued in magical work, as they're filled with possibility and change, and they allow us to be in two realms at once while also not being fully in either one.) It's the moment when the sun is reborn and the darkness gives way to the light. It's a perfect time for magic and meditation related to new beginnings and expanded possibilities.

Noon is the sun's pinnacle. As the brightest point of the bright half of the day, it's not the most popular choice for magical work, which often benefits from more mysterious and liminal qualities of light. Still, it can be useful for magic related to shining light into darkness and all forms of illumination, such as solving mysteries, fostering beneficial connections, and healing old wounds.

Sunset, as the portal between brightness and the dark, supports healing, release, and an appreciative assessment of energies spent. It's a time that can help us make peace with endings of all varieties, and also celebrate how hard we've worked and how far we've come.

Days of the Week

For millennia, spiritual and magical traditions have attributed the qualities of a particular astrological "planet" (astrological planets include the sun and moon, even though they're not technically planets) to each day of the week. Indeed, in many languages (including English), most days contain an etymological reference to a divinity that shares qualities related to (and sometimes even a name with) that planet. And names are powerful! So whether or not you believe that each day of the human-constructed seven-day week contains its own inherent planetary energy, calling them by these divine and planetary names has attuned each day to a particular quality of energy over time.

Sunday is ruled by, and named after, the sun. It's bright, positive, and expansive. It lends itself to magic related to healing, enlightenment, power, and success.

Monday is ruled by, and named after, the moon. It's ethereal, receptive, and deep. It lends itself to magic related to intuition, introspection, nurturing, and relaxation.

Tuesday is ruled by Mars and is named after the Norse god Tyr (Tyr's Old English name was *Tiw*). It's active, competitive, and strong. It lends itself to magic related to victory, activism, and courage.

Wednesday is ruled by Mercury and is named after the Norse god Woden (or Odin). It's quick-witted, communicative, and mobile. It lends itself to magic related to thought, travel, discussion, and the written word.

Thursday is ruled by Jupiter and is named after the Norse god Thor. It's expansive, lucky, and luxurious. It lends itself to magic related to wealth, prosperity, and career.

Friday is ruled by Venus and is named after the Norse goddess Freya (or possibly Frigga). It's romantic, sensual, and aesthetically savvy. It lends itself to magic related to love, beauty, and attraction.

Saturday is ruled by Saturn and named after the Roman god of the same name. It's grounded, practical, and wise. It lends itself to magic related to protection, cleansing, banishing, and the home.

The Sabbats

A year is a day in macrocosm, just as a day is a year in microcosm. For example, just as midnight is both the night's darkest moment and the moment at which the morning is born, the Winter Solstice is both the darkest night of the year and the birth of the light: the moment when the length of the day's brightness begins to grow.

As such, the sabbats (seasonal celebrations) are points of particular power, arranged symmetrically around the wheel of the year. Being aware of these points of power and observing them—in even a small way—helps us align with the magical pulse of Mother Earth as we traverse her miraculous seasonal cycles. (If you're looking for simple ways to celebrate a particular sabbat, you'll find plenty of ideas by searching my blog at www.tesswhitehurst.com. Additionally, Llewellyn, the publisher of this book, has an excellent series of books on each sabbat entitled Llewellyn's Sabbat Essentials.)

Winter Solstice (or Yule)

The Winter Solstice falls around December 22 in the Northern Hemisphere and June 21 in the Southern Hemisphere.

As already mentioned, this is the moment when the light is born. In other words, the days stop growing shorter and begin to grow longer. Spiritually, this is a time for celebrating light within darkness: lighting candles and fireplaces, enjoying fiery herbs such as ginger and cinnamon, and warming our hearts by gathering with friends and family.

Magical work at this time of year might include celebrating what you've learned, experienced, and created in the time since the previous Winter Solstice, bolstering your sense of community and support by feeling gratitude for your loved ones, and setting intentions for the fresh new cycle ahead.

Imbolc

Imbolc is celebrated on February 1 in the Northern Hemisphere and August 1 in the Southern Hemisphere.

Roughly halfway between the Winter Solstice and the Spring Equinox, this is the earliest stirring of spring. Even if the sprouts and flowers haven't yet appeared, we can feel the days growing longer and brighter and sense that spring is getting ready to dawn.

Spiritual work at this time of year might include divination, dream magic, purification, and energizing your spirit by meditating with candles and fire.

Spring Equinox (or Ostara)

The Spring Equinox falls around March 20 in the Northern Hemisphere and September 22 in the Southern Hemisphere.

As indicated by the word *equinox*, this is a time when the days and nights are of roughly equal length and is the halfway point between the solstices. As such, this is a time when we celebrate balance of all varieties. It's also a time of fertility and birth, which is why rabbits, eggs, baby birds, seeds, and sprouts are symbols of this holiday.

Magic for Ostara often includes choosing the qualities and conditions you'd like to give birth to, as well as the areas of life to which you'd like to bring greater balance and harmony.

Beltane (aka Mayday)

Beltane falls on May 1 in the Northern Hemisphere and October 31 in the Southern Hemisphere.

It seems that many witches of old had great fun at Beltane, celebrating and blessing the fertility of the land by dancing around the Maypole (a phallic symbol of great positivity and luck) and then frolicking freely by firelight throughout the night. This is a time when the veil between the realms of human and fairy is the thinnest. Perhaps that's why it seduces us into getting in touch with our rowdy, less domesticated roots. (A secular incarnation of this tradition is still very much present in our culture today. We call it spring break.)

Appropriate magic for Beltane includes dancing, laughing, and frolicking (all of which transform and free up stuck energy), jumping over small bonfires to enliven and purify our personal energy, and spending quality barefoot time outside communing with the fairies (aka nature spirits), flowers, and trees.

Summer Solstice (also called Litha and Midsummer)

The Summer Solstice falls around June 21 in the Northern Hemisphere and December 22 in the Southern Hemisphere.

This is the day when the sun reaches its pinnacle: the longest and brightest day of the year. This makes it a day of great power, as we soak up the magical, healing energy of the sun. Paradoxically, it's also the moment when the dark half of the year is born and the daylight begins to wane. So it can be a time of releasing and letting go of that which we no longer desire or need.

The Summer Solstice is often observed by waking up before the sunrise in order to reverently perceive its emergence on the day of its annual zenith. You might have a cup of tea with the sun. Offer it a libation as it rises (pour it onto the earth in the sun's honor) and give it a toast of gratitude before drinking your own. Then soak in its life-giving rays as you feel it blessing you with the full expansion of its bright positivity and luck.

Lughnasadh (or Lammas)

Lughnasadh is celebrated on August 1 in the Northern Hemisphere and February 1 in the Southern Hemisphere. It's pronounced "Loo-NAH-suh."

The first of three harvest festivals, this is a day of gratitude for the first fruits and grains of the season. The fields and meadows are warm, green, and lush, reminding us that we are perfectly nourished by the abundant blessings of the earth.

Symbolically, all the harvest festivals can be interpreted as times to celebrate the fruits of our labors, whatever they may be. On Lughnasadh, be sure to stop and appreciate how hard you've worked and all your many and varied successes, no matter how big or small.

Fall Equinox (or Mabon)

The Fall Equinox falls around September 22 in the Northern Hemisphere and March 20 in the Southern Hemisphere.

Often the time when we feel that we've entered fall in earnest, this is a celebration of the season: the multicolored meadows, apple orchards, and pumpkin patches. It's a time of beginning to go within as we continue to descend into the darker, more introspective time of year. It's also the second point on the wheel of the year when the days and nights are of roughly equal length and the halfway point between the solstices. We can draw upon this astronomical balance to bring balance to our emotions, relationships, and life conditions.

Spiritually, this is an excellent time to express gratitude for all our good fortune and to bless our hard work as well as the fruits of our labor.

Samhain (aka Halloween)

Samhain falls on October 31 in the Northern Hemisphere and May 1 in the Southern Hemisphere. It's pronounced "SAH-win."

By far the most famous of the sabbats, Samhain is the time when the veil between the worlds of the living and the dead is the thinnest. Similarly, as the last harvest festival, this is the time when we harvest the final fruits and grains and prepare for all the leaves to fall and all the colors to turn to brown.

Magically, this is an opportune time to create altars honoring our deceased family members and friends, make contact with our loved ones on the other side, and make peace with the natural cycle of birth and death.

A New (Ancient) Time Paradigm

You'll find honoring and dancing with time to be a most enjoyable pursuit. It's quite different from the way we often hear time described: the constant striving to beat the clock, kill time, manage time, or find enough time in the day. If you think about it, it's unlikely our ancient ancestors were in conflict with time in this way. Rather, a conflict with time probably wouldn't have made any sense to them. After all, why should you be in conflict with something you're dancing with?

Interestingly, relatively modern scientific thought is beginning to catch up to the ancient time paradigm. According to Einstein, none of us is separate from time: time is emanating from *each of us individually*. In other words, your perception of time is literally dependent upon the unique point of your consciousness in space.

As a matter of fact, the idea that time is outside of us has been effectively debunked by modern science: it's based on an out-moded Newtonian paradigm. As such, psychologist and author Gay Hendricks coined the term *Einstein time* to describe a new way of relating to time. It's based on the fact that Einstein's theory indicates that we are (each and every one of us) time's master—not the other way around. In other words, how much time we have directly correlates with how much time we choose to believe in, expect, and perceive.

Stepping into your magical power means releasing the belief that you're a slave to anyone or anything, including time. This may sound radical and even confusing at first, but if you try it out, you'll begin to understand. In addition to the more long-term practices of dancing with the astrological energies at work throughout the year, try on the paradigm that you are a master of time for just one day. Choose to believe that you always have plenty of time for everything you want to do, and see what happens.

· YOUR MAGIC ·

Get Acquainted with the Magic of the Day

May you live all the days of your life.
~ JONATHAN SWIFT

Every morning for the next seven days, work with an astrological almanac or do web searches to determine the following aspects for each day. Then record them in a journal, notebook, or planner.

- Moon phase (dark, new, waxing, full, or waning?)
- Sun sign
- Moon sign
- Day of the week

Next, look back over this chapter and examine the energies at work for each of the four aspects you noted. Then simply keep them in mind as you go about your day.

At the end of each day, revisit what you wrote while reflecting on what you experienced. Jot down some perceptions: where and how did you see these aspects showing up in your inner and outer worlds?

6

Working with Energy

Consciously interacting with the subtle, invisible realm is a defining behavior of both the quantum physicist and the magic worker. In fact, pretty much every magical activity is some form of energy work, from healing to casting spells to accessing psychic information.

This chapter is a crash course in energy work, designed to give you the solid framework you need to boldly continue along the spiraling, scintillating journey of your magical spiritual path.

The Aura

We are made of energy, and electricity courses through us at all times. *Aura* is simply a synonym for "personal energy field" or "electrical emanation," and chances are very good that you've been sensing auras all your life. For example, have you ever described someone as having "good vibes" or being "a little bit shady"? You were quite probably sensing their energetic qualities: qualities that are obvious to you, yet are not based on input from any of the five usual senses. Even labeling an attractive person you meet as "hot" is often a description of the energetic attraction you feel between your aura and theirs.

For magical purposes, you can think of your aura as a sphere of light that includes your physical body and emanates outward in all directions. Thinking of your physical body as the whole of your "self" is sort of like saying that the candlewick is the flame. You may not always see auras with your physical eyes, but if all you saw was energy (which is all there really is), then a dynamic pool of radiant light is likely how we'd all appear.

It can be useful to get in the habit of tuning in to auras regularly, both your own and those of others. This way, over time, you will awaken to a whole bunch of useful information, including the following:

- The underlying energetic qualities of physical and emotional challenges
- Whom it is safe to trust and whom it is not
- Details about other people's thoughts, feelings, and intentions
- How to naturally heal yourself and others by shifting vibrations

To tune in to an aura—your own or someone else's—simply set the intention to do so and then "look" with your mind's eye. What do you sense? Is the aura very bright and strong, or patchy and thin? Do you sense any dark areas? Any colors, emotions, or other qualities? At first, you might feel like you're making it all up, but if you stick to it, you'll begin to trust what you sense, and even to shift it. After all, our thoughts and emotions are powerful energy influencers.

To experiment with shifting energy, try holding your left hand in front of you, palm up. Envision glowing pink light radiating from the center of your palm. When you can sense your hand shining brightly with light, place it over your heart. Now hold your right hand in front of you, palm up. Envision glowing white light radiating from it, and then place it over your lower belly. Breathe deeply and relax as you take some time to send love and positivity to your heart and belly. Let these areas relax and open as you mentally flood them with healing, balancing light.

Continue until you intuitively feel that your experiment is complete. Notice how different you feel.

The Chakras

According to both ancient and modern energy healers, there are some standard ways that energy swirls and flows through your aura. The main flow of energy, or central meridian, flows both upward and downward along your spinal column, from your tailbone to the crown of your head. To picture how this works, imagine a tree. Nutrients flow into a tree trunk in two ways: upward from the earth and downward from the sky.

Within this central meridian, there are seven main centers where energy swirls and radiates with particular energetic qualities: these are your chakras. Each of these chakras is associated with its own color, as well as unique aspects of your body, mind, spirit, and life conditions.

Orienting yourself to your chakra system is both empowering and enlightening. It allows you to check into your energetic landscape in order to heal and shift all manner of things, including your life patterns and all aspects of your holistic wellbeing.

Here's an overview of the chakra system.

Root Chakra

The root chakra is located at your tailbone. When you sit on the ground or a chair with your spine straight, it's the part of your tailbone that feels the connection between your body and the earth or chair beneath you. Think of it as a horizontally spinning, ruby-red wheel of light. Like the base of a tree, this is where nourishing, supportive earth energy enters your body and aura.

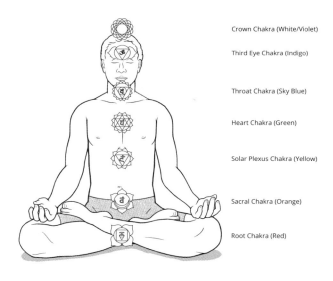

Crown Chakra (White/Violet)

Third Eye Chakra (Indigo)

Throat Chakra (Sky Blue)

Heart Chakra (Green)

Solar Plexus Chakra (Yellow)

Sacral Chakra (Orange)

Root Chakra (Red)

When your root chakra is balanced and activated, you feel grounded, safe, nourished, and comfortably supported by a community of family and / or friends.

Sacral Chakra

The sacral chakra is located at your lower belly area. Think of it as a vertically spinning, vibrant orange wheel of light. Your personal connection to the ocean and the earth's flowing water, this area is aligned with your fluidity and flow.

When your sacral chakra is balanced and activated, you take joy in your senses and your sexuality. You feel comfortable with your whole being, and you naturally take action on your unique creative impulses in ways that feel fun to you.

Solar Plexus Chakra

The solar plexus chakra is located at your upper belly area, at and above your bellybutton. Think of it as a vertically spinning, sun-shiny yellow wheel of light. The center of your energetic solar system, this chakra is very much like your very own sun.

When your solar plexus chakra is balanced and activated, you feel empowered to live the life of your dreams, take up space in the world, and effect positive change according to your will.

Heart Chakra

The heart chakra is right in the middle of your chest, at your emotional center: the place that feels both grief and love. Think of it as a vertically spinning ball of radiant emerald green light. When you breathe into this chakra, which is aligned with the air element, you connect with your own sweetness and precious sensitivity. Healing this area infuses your life with lightness and joy, like a sparkling sunrise.

When your heart chakra is balanced and activated, you feel loved, loving, and lovable. Your emotions are open and flowing, and you feel a heart-centered connection to everyone you meet.

Throat Chakra

The throat chakra is in the center of your neck area. Think of it as a vertically spinning wheel of sky-blue light. When this chakra is healthy, its energy is very much like a clear mountain lake sparkling in sunlight.

When your throat chakra is balanced and activated, clear and creative communication flows from you effortlessly. You feel comfortable speaking your truth and embarking on meaningful creative endeavors, and you do both with love.

Third Eye Chakra

The third eye chakra is in the center of your forehead. Think of it as a small, vertically spinning wheel of luminescent indigo light. This is the place where you see through the eyes of spirit and perceive the subtle energetic patterns that define and animate all things.

When your third eye chakra is balanced and activated, your intuition is a natural part of your life. You perceive the world through your five senses, but also through a sixth, subtler sense that provides valuable inspiration and insight.

Crown Chakra

The crown chakra is at the top of your head. Think of it as a horizontally spinning wheel of white and/or violet light, like a ceiling fan at the crown of your head. This is the place where your finite self interacts with infinity, and divine energy and information flow down into your energetic field from the cosmos.

When your crown chakra is balanced and activated, you feel naturally joyful and at one with All That Is. You are constantly refreshed and purified by an infinite flow of divine energy and love.

• ● •

Using these descriptions, you can examine your current qualities of wellbeing to get an initial read on which of your chakras are in harmony and which may need a little work. Additionally, there are often physical cues. For example, a sacral chakra issue may manifest as severe menstrual cramps or digestive issues, and if you have migraine headaches regularly, it's likely that your third eye chakra is blocked.

If you determine that one of your chakras could use some special attention, try this simple chakra-healing exercise.

A Simple Chakra-Healing Exercise

Go someplace where you won't be disturbed, and sit or recline comfortably, with your spine relatively straight. Close your eyes and begin to breathe consciously, allowing your breath to naturally deepen. Lovingly notice any tense areas in your body, and imagine that you're breathing into them one by one, letting the breath naturally soothe and relax each area.

When you feel very relaxed, move your attention to the chakra you want to heal. Breathe into it. See it bathed in very bright white light. As you breathe in, feel the air opening the chakra, and as you breathe out, sense the chakra spinning faster, getting brighter, and throwing off any dark, challenging, or stuck energy, which instantly dissolves in the bright light of spirit. Continue this breathing visualization until you feel the tension release and the whole chakra area come into greater harmony and balance.

Once this feels complete, see if you can tune in to the wisdom of the chakra. Does it have any messages for you about how to bring your life into greater harmony? For example, if it's your solar plexus chakra, it's likely to have a message about how to own and express your personal power more harmoniously. This message may arrive as a word, an image, or an unmistakable inner knowing. When the message has been fully communicated, thank your chakra for alerting you to the imbalance, and vow to act on the guidance you've received. While it's still fresh in your mind, jot it down in a journal if you'd like. Repeat this process as necessary.

As a magic worker, cultivating and maintaining a clear, vibrant, and positive energy field is an important prerequisite. Value it highly and prioritize it. It's similar to the way physical fitness is extremely important for everyone, but it's *vitally* important for gymnasts and ballerinas. Magical people are like gymnasts and ballerinas of energy. That's why a solid daily habit of clearing, activating, and shielding your aura and chakras is absolutely essential. (I call this *magical hygiene*, and the next section is all about it.)

Magical Hygiene

As a professional magical person, I get a lot of questions from readers and students about how to solve all kinds of problems, magical and mundane. And a large percentage of them could have been prevented (and often can still be solved) by a solid magical hygiene practice. Let me be very clear: good magical hygiene is absolutely essential for everyone embarking on a magical spiritual practice. Here's why:

- Like attracts like. When we cultivate and maintain a positive vibration, we attract positive conditions, relationships, and experiences.

- Working with energy on a regular basis opens us up to the subtle reality, which contains the whole spectrum of energetic conditions, including challenging vibrations from things like negative emotions, ego-based intentions, and unsavory entities. Magical hygiene allows us to choose which frequencies are allowed into our personal energy field and which are not.

- Those of us who are drawn to magic are often extremely sensitive because of childhood conditions where we felt unsafe and learned to pick up on vibrations as a survival mechanism. While these traumas led to the cultivation of our intuitive and energetic superpowers, they also often mean that we can use some help in the boundary department. Magical hygiene is a powerful method of establishing healthy personal boundaries.

- Our energetic wellbeing underlies and defines our emotional and physical wellbeing. By keeping our chakras balanced and our aura clear, we powerfully support our holistic wellbeing.

- Emanating a positive spiritual vibration (as we do when we have a solid magical hygiene practice) has an amazingly positive effect on everyone we love, everyone we encounter, and everyone in our physical vicinity. In fact, if you think of everything as energy, it's like we're broadcasting waves of positivity across the entire unified field.

But just what *is* magical hygiene? It's pretty simple. At first the practice might seem a bit involved, but once you get the hang of it, you can fit it into just five to ten minutes or so. Here's how to do it.

···················· YOUR MAGIC ·····················
Energy Clearing and Energizing

Once a day, preferably before you leave the house and get busy with all your activities, sit comfortably, with your spine straight. You might sit cross-legged on a cushion (possibly in front of your altar), or you can just sit in a chair, with your feet flat on the floor. Breathe consciously. Notice when your breath goes in and when it goes out. Allow it to naturally deepen. Also notice any part of your body where you're holding tension, and allow it to relax.

When you feel centered and present, call on Archangel Michael and Archangel Raphael to clear your aura completely.* Ask them to remove any cords of attachment (i.e., unhealthy energetic connections to other people or conditions) and any stuck or challenging vibrations. You might envision them with a glowing vacuum tube of light that moves through your energy field, powerfully removing anything other than pure, vibrant positivity and light.

Then ask them to completely fill and surround you with a sphere of blindingly bright golden-white light, in which only love remains and through which only love may enter. Remember that this life experience is an illusion, and that only love is real: an eternal, supportive interconnection between you and All That Is. So this is not a way of pushing anything away, but rather a way of recognizing the truth of everything, which is always love. In this way, you might imagine the shield of light to be permeable, like actual light, but when anything other than love comes through (i.e., the illusion of separation and discord), it is completely transformed and transmuted into love.

Now that you're safely cocooned in positivity and love, imagine you are sending roots of light down into the earth from your tailbone and legs. Like a tree, extend your roots downward, but keep going until you reach the core of the earth, which you can envision as a glowing subterranean sun. Allow your roots to plug into this earth light and drink it up. Sense the light naturally coming up your roots, much like electricity flows through a cord once it's plugged into an outlet. Allow this earth light to reach your body and flow though your entire energy field.

Next, send a trunk of light upward from the crown of your head. Again like a tree, let your trunk and branches reach upward for nourishment, but continue reaching up until you exit the earth's atmosphere and connect with the infinite, clear light of the cosmos. Let your branches plug into this light, and sense it moving down your trunk and into the crown of your head, your body, and your entire energy field. See and sense it merging with the earth light.

Take a moment now to connect with each chakra, and to imagine and sense the earth light and the cosmic light cleansing, activating, and balancing each one. Start with your root chakra, then move up to your sacral chakra, your solar plexus chakra, your heart chakra, your throat chakra, your third eye chakra, and your crown chakra.

Finally, take some time to infuse your day and life with joyful success. If you can really feel the feelings associated with the conditions you'd most like to experience, you'll be tuning your radio dial to their frequency and thereby drawing them toward you like a magnet. Do your best to feel gratitude for these conditions, as if they are already 100 percent present and true.

* In my personal experience, Archangel Michael and Archangel Raphael are the best helpers I've found for the purpose of clearing energy. They are powerful higher-ups in the angelic hierarchy. Michael is aligned with protection and the fire element, and Raphael with healing and the air element. If you want to call on different helpers or simply "divine light," feel free to adapt the practice accordingly. If you'd like to learn more about angels and how to work with them, the book *Angel Therapy* by Doreen Virtue is a good place to start.

Environmental Energetics

Enclosed spaces, such as our homes and workplaces, tend to hold energetic patterns in place. This can have a profound effect on every aspect of our life experience, particularly if we spend time in them regularly. But you can easily shift these patterns and improve the vibration of interior spaces in the following ways:

- **Clear clutter.** Do you love it, use it, or need it? Or, in the words of bestselling author and tidying expert Marie Kondo, "Does it spark joy?" If not, donate it, recycle it, or throw it away.

- **Clean.** As you can probably sense every time you walk into a freshly cleaned room, physical cleaning clears energy right along with the dust. Cleanliness is next to Goddessness.

- **Decorate only with imagery that uplifts and inspires you.** Art with negative or heavy imagery is fine in a museum or gallery, but if you see it day in and day out, it will have an undesirable effect on your energy as well as the conversations and relationship dynamics that take place in the space.

- **Make noise.** Clapping, banging a drum, or using a rattle can break up stuck energy, and soothing music (like classical or New Age) sends sacred geometric energetic patterns throughout the space, shifting energy at the molecular level. Chanting affirmations or mantras has a similarly positive effect.

- **Clear the energy with herbs.** The old standby space-clearing herb is white sage. It's commonly tied into a bundle and dried, and is sold at many metaphysical supply stores. If you burn white sage in your space, make sure to blow out the flame so that it's smoking like incense, and then carry a dish under it to catch any burning embers. Move in a counterclockwise direction throughout each room and area, allowing the smoke to waft around the room, making a clean sweep as it instantly clears all negative vibrations and transmutes them into love. Alternatives to white sage include desert sage, palo santo wood, and smudge spray, which can all be employed in similar ways. (Find smudge sprays on Etsy, or make your own by adding ten to twenty drops of essential oil of sage, clary sage, cedar, and/or lavender to a mister of spring water.)

······················· YOUR MAGIC ·······················
Establish a Magical Hygiene Practice
As portals between the inner and outer worlds, the chakra system gives us a map to heal not just ourselves, but the world we share.
~ ANODEA JUDITH, *CHAKRAS*

Starting now and for at least the remainder of your study of this book (but ideally forever), do the magical hygiene meditation ("Energy Clearing and Energizing") from earlier in this chapter. It's fine if you adapt it or allow it to change over time as you find what works best for you. I find it's best to do it in the morning, but if it's easier for you to do it in the evening, that's fine too. The important thing is that you do it—pretty much every day.

If you skip a day (or a month), though, all is not lost. As with any good habit you want to establish, if you've fallen off the wagon, just show up and do it again, no matter how long it's been.

After practicing good magical hygiene for as little as a week, you'll notice highly positive effects. In time, you'll think of it like brushing your teeth: you might leave the house without doing it sometimes, but that's the exception rather than the rule.

7

Reading the Signs

Your awareness of the subtle realm makes you a wise one. Whether or not you realize it, you *know things*. You have the ability to see, sense, or feel into the invisible patterns and possibilities, which can give you insight into what to do, what not to do, and how to best proceed.

There are many ways this gift can appear. Maybe you've consciously experienced one or more of them already. Or maybe you've never noticed that you possess such a talent, so now you're starting to worry that you're not actually magical after all.

If this is the case, cut it out!

Let me draw your attention to the fact that you are now on chapter 7. So chances are good you're *fairly* sure I'm not crazy, and the information in this book resonates with you at least a little. Of course, I truly believe that deep down, everyone has vast magical potential, but those who are not quite ready to own their spiritual gifts will have returned this book to the library or thrown it in the recycling bin by this point. The evidence backs me up when I say:

you have intuitive abilities that you've probably been drawing upon all your life without even realizing it.

If you think about it, it's kind of natural that you wouldn't be able to easily recognize your own intuitive abilities at first. To use myself as an example, throughout my life I've often felt other people's emotions almost as clearly as my own, so I assumed this was something that happened to everyone. I still find it hard to believe that the broadcasts that are coming through loud and clear on my emotional radio are just about nonexistent to a large percentage of humans.

It's sort of like how my extremely musically talented boyfriend Ted seems to believe that everyone can sing and play the guitar. These things come so naturally to him that whenever someone says they can't do one or both of them, he thinks they're just deluding themselves or psyching themselves out. I've heard him express this belief on more than one occasion, and I've never been able to talk him out of it.

Similarly (if you're not already aware of your intuitive gifts), there is almost certainly something you assume that everyone can perceive that is actually a perception that is relatively unique to you.

In the next section, you'll find descriptions of some of the most commonly experienced intuitive abilities, as well as fun experiments to allow you to experience each one. See if you can identify one or more abilities that you might possess. (Hint: it's a major clue if you find yourself thinking, "Well, sure, I can do that, but that's not intuition; it's just a totally normal thing I do. Everybody does that, right?")

I suggest that you read through every description and experiment, even if you don't think you possess the gift as described. As you assimilate the information over the coming days and weeks, you may be surprised to suddenly recognize the presence of a gift you didn't think you had. In fact, there's a good chance you will eventually be able to access every single one of these gifts to some extent.

The Primary Intuitive Gifts

Seeing

Some magical folk see subtle and otherworldly energy with their physical eyes. They see things like auras, angels, spirits, and qualities of energy, such as a bright quality of joy or dark areas in the body that indicate illness or physical pain. Others see these same things in the form of pictures that arise in their mind. When this gift is consciously activated, many are able to see situations, people, and objects in their mind's eye in order to detect images, patterns, colors, and/or symbols that can be interpreted to provide helpful insight and guidance.

> *Experiment:* Close your eyes. In your mind's eye, look at your heart chakra, the wheel of emotional energy in the center of your chest. What do you see? Brightness? Color? Any sort of image, pattern, or symbol? Take some time to discern what your inner vision is telling you about the current state of your emotions and heart.

Knowing

Do you ever "just know" something, without being able to explain exactly *how* you know? For example, when you hear your phone ding, do you just know who's texting you? Or perhaps when you meet someone, you just know they're a surfer, or a vegan, or that they went through a divorce recently or love the Lord of the Rings trilogy. Even if this sort of thing happens to you only once in a while, it's still an indication of an intuitive gift.

Experiment: For the next twenty-four hours, every time your phone dings, see if you "just know" who it is.

Feeling

As I mentioned previously in the personal example, some of us can feel the emotions of others. If this is one of your gifts, then simply sitting next to someone on the bus or in a movie theater can cause you to feel that person's emotions. Additionally, you might be able to "feel" the emotions of people or animals you see in photos, or even loved ones who may be many miles away. Naturally, crowds and big cities can often be challenging for folks with this gift, as it can feel like way too much energy and emotion to process all at once.

Please note that before this gift is integrated in a healthy way, you may find it painful and confusing to absorb emotions from every which way, not always knowing where your emotions end and those of others begin. But if you keep up with the magical hygiene practice from the previous chapter, you'll not only be able to protect yourself from negativity but you'll also be able to clearly discern what emotions are coming from whom and to emanate supportive compassion without drowning in the pain.

Experiment: Go outside and spend some time with a healthy plant or tree. Open up to the "emotions" of the plant, and allow yourself to receive an infusion of its vitality and calm.

Hearing

Have you ever "heard" guidance in your mind in the form of a word or a complete sentence? Recently, I was seriously considering purchasing a gorgeous amethyst pendant from a vendor in the lobby outside a belly dance show. Then, in my mind, I clearly heard the sentence "That pendant isn't for you." Later, while in line to get in, I saw a woman wearing that exact pendant, looking absolutely radiant. It was unmistakably *her* pendant. The harmonic resonance between the necklace and the necklace's ideal owner had translated itself into the firm but loving message for me to move along.

Some of us also perceive the presence of otherworldly spirits in a home through a certain quality of sound, or gain insight into the lives and intentions of others through the quality of their voice.

When this gift is powerfully activated, you may intuitively hear sounds (songs, chimes, words, etc.) with your physical ears.

Experiment: For the next twenty-four hours, every time you listen to someone speak, see if you can "hear" any words behind their words. Is there something they're saying that they're not actually speaking aloud?

Touching

If you are able to learn a lot by simply reaching out and touching something, then this is certainly one of your gifts. Magical people with this gift are likely to walk through a secondhand store with their hands in their pockets, and to pick something up only if they actually might want to buy it. Then, once they do pick it up, the information they receive through their hands may be the deciding factor, because it will give them an idea of where the item has been, whom it's been with, and what kind of accompanying energy it will bring into their home.

Experiment: Visit a bookstore and use your hands to choose a book. See if you can feel the energy in your palms guiding you toward a certain section, and then, without looking at the titles, run your hands along the spines of the books until you reach the one that feels right. Does it seem like something you would like, or does it feel significant in some way?

Smelling

Finally, let's discuss the intuitive sense that generally gets the least attention: smell. Many of us "smell" things with our mind's nose. For example, the presence of a deceased loved one on the other side may be indicated by a particular scent, such as cigarettes, roses, or freshly baked cookies. If you're like me, when you consciously connect with the angelic realm, you may sometimes notice the scent of sweet-smelling white flowers such as jasmine and gardenia. Or the memory of a certain scent may unexpectedly arise while you are considering an important decision, providing a vital insight, tipoff, or clue.

> *Experiment:* If there's something important you're considering, intuitively open up to assigning a scent to each option. Ask yourself: If I were to choose this option, how would it smell? Then do the same with the additional option(s). It may not seem to make sense, but moving to Austin might smell like cinnamon rolls, while moving to Denver might smell like rice vinegar. Once you recognize this, you can take some time to tune in to what these scents may mean for you. Maybe they provide insight into how you feel in your heart of hearts about each potential path. Or maybe they're foretelling that you'll open a bakery if you move to Austin and a sushi restaurant if you move to Denver. (Alas, intuition is not an exact science. But over time we can get more proficient with our own unique gifts, provided we practice them regularly.)

Oracle Cards

When it's your intention to tap into a clear wellspring of intuitive guidance, oracle cards can be invaluable. Like tarot cards, these are decks of cards created specifically for the purpose of tuning in to divine wisdom and your own inner knowing. Unlike with tarot cards, you need not devote hours of study in order to perform a solid reading with oracle cards. Their wisdom is (generally) instantly accessible to all.

If you don't already have an oracle deck you like, some good introductory decks include the *Goddess Guidance Oracle Cards* by Doreen Virtue, *Whispers of Lord Ganesha* by Angela Hartfield, and my own deck, the *Magic of Flowers Oracle*.

Each oracle deck is different, so once you find one you like, perform readings according to the instructions in the accompanying book. (They almost always come with a little book.) However, a common method that will work with most decks is as follows:

1. Phrase your question clearly, in an open-ended way. Instead of asking a yes-or-no question, such as "Should I move to Austin?" you might say, "Please give me insight into my potential move to Austin."

2. Shuffle the deck. Continue shuffling until it feels right to stop. (Note that there is no way you can mess this up—whenever you stop is perfect.)

3. Taking from the top of the deck, deal three cards, faceup, from left to right.

4. The first card is the past, the second card is the present, and the third card is the future. You might also think of the first card as being the foundation of or motivating factors behind

the issue, the second card as being descriptive of the main challenge or primary energy of the experience, and the third card as being where the issue is presently taking you or what you are learning from it.

5. Begin by just looking at the images and getting a feel for them. What messages do they seem to be giving you? What stories do they tell you about your life and the situation you're asking about?

6. Take a moment to read the descriptions of each card, noticing if any specific sentences or words stand out to you.

The Tarot

The tarot is a powerful divinatory system involving archetypal characters, stories, and life experiences. While there are thousands of different decks with extremely diverse imagery and descriptions, tarot decks hold to the same general format. What sets the tarot apart from oracle decks is that the tarot can give you insight into the ancient stories and character roles that are being played out in any given situation, which allows for a deeper level of understanding of the grander scope of things. You might say that while oracle cards can help us answer the questions "What direction should I take?" and "What is the lesson here?" tarot cards are more suited to helping us answer the questions "What is going on?" and "What is the underlying pattern at work here?"

While a single book or class can get you started on reading tarot cards immediately, the study of tarot can last a lifetime, as we spiral ever more deeply into the vast wisdom that it holds.

If you're not familiar with tarot, and you'd like to be (it's certainly not a requirement), my suggestion is to find a deck that really speaks to you. I found it difficult to connect with the tarot for years, until I finally found the *Witches Tarot* by Ellen Dugan. With the help of this deck, the tarot suddenly came to life for me. You may have the same experience with the *Witches Tarot*, or the deck that clicks for you may be something else entirely. Take time to find one with images and descriptions that are profoundly inspiring to you. Then let your enthusiasm for the deck propel your study of each card's image and meaning as you practice reading the cards as described in the accompanying book.

Once you've begun your tarot journey in this way, continue to let your eagerness light your path. Find books, websites, or classes that spark your interest, or just continue to work and meditate with the cards themselves.

The I Ching

The I Ching is over two thousand years old, and is in fact the oldest of the Chinese classics. Like the tarot, the I Ching (which translates to *Book of Changes*) is a complete system of divination that can help you understand the intricate inner dynamics of any given situation, as well as the wisest ways to proceed. Also like the tarot, there are many versions of the I Ching, which differ greatly from one another on the surface but possess the same basic structure.

In ancient times, yarrow stalks were often used to access the divinatory wisdom of the I Ching, but these days many I Ching readers use three shiny coins, such as pennies or dimes.

The I Ching translation that I personally prefer is Stephen Karcher's *Total I Ching*, but I've found that everyone must find their own favorite. There's no telling which one will be best for you. And, of course, the I Ching might not be your thing at all! But if you're intrigued, follow the same instructions I gave for learning the tarot: find one you like, and then work with it as described in the accompanying book, letting your natural enthusiasm lead the way.

Pendulums

For years and years I shied away from using a pendulum. Today it's hands down my most frequently used magical tool. This is a good example of following what you're drawn to and what works best for you personally, and being open to letting this change over the years.

You can find pendulums at most metaphysical supply shops, but you can also just use a pendant, or tie any weighted object (such as a bead or washer) to the end of a string. Indeed, when I can't find my pendulum, I've been known to use whatever I find lying around: a tea cozy, a necklace, or even (if I truly can't do any better) my phone charger.

When using a pendulum, remember that it's not moving on its own. The energy behind its movement is coming through *you*, from your own arm and hand. You're effectively allowing your body to be a channel of divine wisdom and your own inner knowing. Like all methods of divination, it's a way of bypassing your linear, thinking mind and accessing the current of divine wisdom and information that knows and understands all. This current is absolutely within you and is naturally accessible to you. And when you use a pendulum, you witness firsthand that it's an *actual* current, like a sound current or a current of electricity.

Generally, pendulums work by answering with an affirmative or a negative, like a person who nods *yes* or shakes their head *no*. But it's important to remember that divine wisdom is not the same as intellectual human thinking. For example, the future is not set: there are countless possibilities before one is singled out and realized. So your answer will not be reliable if you ask a pendulum a yes-or-no question, such as "Is this person going to call me tomorrow?"

What the pendulum does work well for is the following:

• Validating intuitive hits

• Validating preferences (i.e., noticing which choices will support your energy and which will do nothing for it or will even deplete it)

• Refining messages received through other intuitive tools such as the tarot and oracle decks

• Discovering which chakras are open and which are blocked

• Helping you tune in to what your body most wants to eat and drink before a meal, or what dietary supplements are best for you at any given time

Be careful when asking the pendulum a question to which you really want a particular answer. In these cases, in addition to asking your question, you may be unwittingly reciting (or nonverbally emitting the energy of) a phrase such as "please say yes, please say yes." In such a case, your pendulum will certainly oblige, but it may not be responding to what you think it's responding to. So while we humans use words to tune in and ask questions, oracular tools respond to the energy behind the question. This is a good example of the importance of first getting clear about your intention and then getting your energy in alignment with your intention. (This is vital not just in divination but in all magical work.)

To get started with a pendulum, take a moment to harmonize with it. Cup it in your right hand, and lightly place your left hand over it. Breathe, relax, and visualize/feel/sense it filled and pulsating with vibrant divine light. Then hold it with your right hand so the weighted portion is hanging straight down. Say (or think), "Show me *yes*." While relaxing your elbow and arm (and not holding them rigid), allow the pendulum to swing in the pattern it naturally seems to want to go. For many people, a *yes* answer is a forward-and-backward motion or a clockwise circle, but be open to whatever you notice. Then say, "Show me *no.*" Again, look for the pattern in which the pendulum naturally wants to swing. A *no* answer is often a side-to-side motion or a counterclockwise circle, but again it might be different for you.

Dreams and Omens

We all have strange and fascinating dreams. And we all have times when we notice a certain animal, symbol, or number sequence popping up again and again in our dreams.

There are plenty of books and websites out there on dream interpretation, animals, numbers, and other symbols, and that's great! But you don't need them. You already have access to the divine wisdom that's coming through your dreams and the omens you see in the physical world. After all, these are the Great Holy Mystery's way of communicating with you, and the Great Holy Mystery (aka God/Goddess/All That Is/the part of you that is one with everything) wouldn't use a language you don't understand. To decipher the code, all you have to do is take a moment and ask yourself this: *"If I had to guess* what that dream meant (or why I keep seeing raccoons everywhere, or what the significance of 11:11 is for me), what would I guess?"

In some cases, your first answer will be "I really don't know." Then just ask yourself again: "Okay, fine. I don't know. But if I absolutely *had* to guess, what would I guess?" Pretty much across the board, your "guess" will be the answer you seek. This is all that is needed to make the jump from linear, language-based *thinking* to multidimensional, energy-based *knowing.*

After that, if you want to, go ahead and look up the dream symbol or the animal totem or whatever. You'll probably see parallels, but you aren't likely to see anything as unique and specific to you as the answer you already uncovered all on your own.

····················· YOUR MAGIC ·······················
Read the Cards

When we experience ourselves as passive victims of change,
we feel cut off, isolated, frightened, and angry. When we are a part
of the dialogue, we feel connected to the basic creative energy
that shapes the world we live in.
~ STEPHEN KARCHER, *TOTAL I CHING*

Visit a mainstream or metaphysical bookstore, online or in person. Take some time to find and purchase an oracle deck that sparks your sense of inspiration and wonder. Bring it home, sit with it near your altar, light a candle, and get to know it. Look at the images. Call on the Divine in a way that feels powerful to you, and earnestly request a blessing for the deck and for all your future intuitive work. Hold the deck to your heart and ask that your readings be clear and your inner wisdom be fully tapped into divine guidance. Then perform a reading or two, being sure to ask the question(s) that you most want to know the answers to in your heart of hearts. You can use the instructions in the "Oracle Cards" section in this chapter, or follow the directions that accompany your deck.

Finally, visit a fabric or craft store and purchase a yard of indigo ribbon. Bless the ribbon by spreading it out in bright sunlight for five to ten minutes. To symbolize your awakening intuition, to further align you with the deck, and to preserve the deck's positivity and power, wind the ribbon around your deck and lovingly tie it with a bow. Unwind it whenever you use the cards, and retie it when you're finished.

8

Casting a Spell

There's something glorious about casting a spell.

While a prayer is a polite request, a spell is an audacious decree. It's not "I humbly ask for this condition if it is in alignment with divine will," it's a bold "My will is divine will! And *as I will it, so shall it be.*" It's a fearless demonstration of this (paraphrased) timeless advice from Henry David Thoreau: "Go confidently in the direction of your dreams. Live the life you have imagined."

Do you wish in your heart of hearts for a certain condition? Create it! Craft it. Bring it into being. Work with the Great Holy Mystery and conjure it right up.

Of course, there's a reason I've written so many chapters before this one, and I sincerely hope you've read them. Chapters 3 and 4 ("Understanding the Dynamics" and "Connecting with Power") in particular contain important prerequisites to spellcasting. For example, for your spell to truly be a success, you must choose an intention that is in alignment with your true, divine nature (not your ego), and you must understand where your power comes from: from the earth, the cosmos, the elements, and All That Is.

To reiterate, your power does *not* come from the seemingly finite you, tooling around for mere decades in this teeny-tiny corner of time and space! And your power is not something to boast about or to use to prop up your ego. Rather, your power is an inherent aspect of the infinite, eternal, expansive you. When you act from this aspect of yourself, you have no reason to brag or convince anyone of your greatness. Why would you, when it is so absolutely certain that you are one with the power that creates worlds?

All that being said, this chapter will give you the coaching you need to get started on your spellwork. I suggest that you read through all the instructions before trying anything, and then put all your knowledge to work when you reach the exercise at the end of the chapter, which is a self-initiation spell. (I know that magic students can feel intimidated when it comes to casting their first spell, but don't worry—I've designed it to be super simple, doable, and fun. You'll love it!)

Calling the Quarters and Casting a Circle

When you're first getting started with spellcasting, it's a good idea to call the quarters and cast a circle every time. Both these actions help ensure success by providing spiritual protection, improving mental and energetic concentration, and connecting you with divine power. Not to mention, every time you do them, you'll be building up your spellworking chops, so you'll be on the fast track to magical virtuosity.

I've outlined the way I, personally, like to call the quarters and cast a circle. You might like to start with this and then adapt it as you get to know your own magical preferences.

If you don't currently have an outdoor area where you can work magic privately (alas, the slightest chance someone might stumble upon us mid-spell can cause us to feel too self-conscious for successful magical work), you'll want to work magic indoors. (It's important that you choose a time and place where you will absolutely not be disturbed.) In this case, a round rug about four to six feet in diameter is a great tool to have, particularly when you're still getting the hang of everything, as it helps you clearly visualize the edge of your magic circle. Otherwise, it can be helpful to mark a similarly sized circle on the floor, using something like scarves, coins, or a spool of ribbon.

Once you've created your circle, use a compass (most smartphones have them as a built-in app) to determine the four cardinal points of the circle: north, south, east, and west. Remember your altar items that symbolize the elements (from the exercise at the end of chapter 4)? You're going to use those to mark the points. At the north, place the item from your altar that symbolizes earth. At the east, place the item that symbolizes air. At the south, place the item that symbolizes fire. And at the west, place the item that symbolizes water. Near each item, place a white or off-white votive, jar candle, or tealight in a holder. (If a four-legged friend will be wandering around, be sure to place the candle in a tall jar or vase in such a way that tails, fur, and whiskers will be safe from fire.) Make sure to have a lighter or matches on your person or inside the circle.

Later in the chapter we'll be talking about casting the spell itself, but for now just keep in mind that if your spell requires physical ingredients or tools of any kind, you'll want to make sure to have them inside the circle before calling the quarters.

Here's how to call the quarters and cast a circle.

Stand comfortably in the center of the circle, facing east. Your spine should be straight in a comfortable way and your legs slightly bent (not locked). Close your eyes and come into the space and the present moment by breathing consciously. Notice when you breathe in and when you breathe out. Allow your breath to naturally deepen as you notice it.

When you feel centered and present, imagine you are sending roots of light down into the earth from your tailbone, legs, and feet. Continue sending your roots down until they reach the core of the earth. (Ideally, you've been practicing something very similar during your magical hygiene practice.) Envision the core of the earth as a golden, subterranean sun. Allow your roots to drink in this anchoring, nourishing light, and sense it naturally flowing up through your entire body and energy field.

Next, send a trunk and branches of light up into the sky from the crown of your head. Continue expanding these upward until you exit the earth's atmosphere and connect with an infinity of white light with rainbow sparkles. Allow your branches to drink in this balancing, all-knowing light, and sense it naturally flowing down through your entire body and energy field, merging and mixing with the earth light.

Say:

Mother Earth, you are here and I thank you.
Father Cosmos, you are here and I thank you.

As you continue to face east, connect with the element of air. Feel it in your lungs and on your skin. Envision a sunrise in the east, a bird flying, and wind in trees.

Say:

Guardians of the east, element of air, I call on you.
You are here and I thank you.

Turn toward the south and connect with the element of fire. Feel the heat of your body and emotions. Envision a desert landscape at noon, with the blazing sun high in the sky and a crackling bonfire raging.

Say:

Guardians of the south, element of fire, I call on you.
You are here and I thank you.

Turn toward the west and connect with the element of water. Feel the moisture in your mouth and flowing through your organs and veins. Envision the ocean at sunset, hear the sound of crashing waves, and feel water rushing around you.

Say:

Guardians of the west, element of water, I call on you.
You are here and I thank you.

Turn toward the north and connect with the element of earth. Feel the solidity of your bones, your body, and the ground on which you stand. Envision a fertile field at midnight, smell the rich earth, and listen to the deep and expansive silence.

Say:

Guardians of the north, element of earth, I call on you.
You are here and I thank you.

Point the index finger of your right hand down toward the edge of the circle. Imagine a laser of white or blue light extending from your finger, then rotate a full 360 degrees, tracing the edge of the circle with this energy as you do so. In your mind's eye, see it appear on the floor like brightly glowing chalk. This will create a container for the energy you raise during your spell while sealing your circle in spiritual protection.

Face east again.

Say:

The circle is cast. We are between the worlds.

Performing the Spell

As you will see in the second half of this book, spells come in many forms. Sometimes they have ingredients and sometimes they don't. Sometimes words are spoken and sometimes they aren't.

The powerful aspect of a spell is never the spell; it's the intention behind the spell and the energy that gets shifted during the spell. The spell is essentially a framework that allows you to focus energy toward your goal and shift energy according to what will help you manifest your goal.

Spells also work because they have a powerful effect on the subconscious mind. As we've seen, our thoughts, feelings, expectations, and beliefs have a huge effect on—and literally create—the conditions we experience. But so many of our thoughts, feelings, expectations, and beliefs are rooted in our subconscious. By definition, this aspect of our mind is not accessible from our everyday consciousness, so it can be extremely difficult to alter it without some way of rappelling into our mind's mysterious, inscrutable depths. Spells can take us there. And they allow us to change the coding that defines our everyday experience.

Whatever spell you choose, do it with lightness, playfulness, and fun. All these qualities keep us open to divine support and pure potentiality. Even if the spell is for something that feels heavy and important (like healing for a loved one or manifesting money for rent), do your best not to take it too seriously, even while feeling a deep sense of reverence and awe. If you forget something or drop something, laugh. It's no big deal. It doesn't have to be an omen. The spell can still work. And don't worry about making some fatal mistake that will bring about undesired consequences. This isn't the movies. As long as you choose an intention that's in alignment with your divine desire (and not your ego), and as long as you call on divine support regularly (as part of your magical hygiene practice and in calling the quarters and casting the circle), you have absolutely nothing to fear.

Thanking the Quarters and Opening the Circle

After you've cast your spell, it's time to thank the quarters and open the circle. This is a way of releasing all that magical energy into the ether. You might think of the spellwork you've done up to this point like writing a letter and putting it in an envelope. When you open the circle, it's like dropping your envelope in the mail and trusting implicitly that it will get to its intended destination. So don't discount the importance of this aspect of the magical work! After all, you can write the most articulate letter in the world, address it in calligraphy, and even stick a special edition Janis Joplin stamp on it, but it all will be to no avail if you never actually drop the envelope in the mail.

Here's how to thank the quarters.

Start by facing west. Connect with the element of water by imagining the sunset and the rushing waves, as you did when you called the quarters. Then say:

Guardians of the west, element of water,
You were here, and I thank you.

Face south. Connect with the element of fire. Say:

Guardians of the south, element of fire,
You were here, and I thank you.

Face east. Connect with the element of air. Say:

Guardians of the east, element of air,
You were here, and I thank you.

Face north. Connect with the element of earth. Say:

Guardians of the north, element of earth,
You were here, and I thank you.

Connect with the earth beneath you and the cosmos above you. Say:

Mother Earth, you were here, and I thank you.
Father Cosmos, you were here, and I thank you.

Feel so much gratitude in your heart as you reflect on how wonderful it is to be able to tap into divine power and manifest the conditions you desire. Feel gratitude for all the support and the beauty around you, from the elements, the earth, the cosmos, and All That Is. Say:

Thank you, thank you, thank you.
Blessed be. And so it is.

As a final expression of releasing the energy, spin in one full counterclockwise circle, and then fling your arms upward to the sky.

Earthing the Power

After working all that magic, you'll have a supernova's worth of extra energy in your aura that you don't need. So you'll want to send it into Mother Earth, who is much better equipped to harmoniously assimilate it into her energy field and will actually benefit from the boost.

Here's how to earth the power.

Start by crouching down and placing your open palms on the floor or earth. Then set the intention to send any and all excess energy back into Mother Earth, while retaining the perfect amount of energy for your everyday purposes. Envision the energy in the form of light flowing out through your palms, down into the ground, and deep into the core of the earth.

Next, if possible, lie flat on the ground on your back for about five minutes or so. (Otherwise, sit in a chair, with your spine straight and your feet flat on the ground.) While in this position, feel the earth beneath you. Become aware of how it feels to be in a body, and reattune your senses to the physical, everyday world.

Finally, it's a good idea to eat some carbohydrates to further reattune yourself to the grounded realm of the day-to-day world. A cookie, toast, pasta, rice, cereal, potatoes, or a granola bar are all good choices. Or, if you're a paleo or raw food enthusiast, a banana, a sweet potato, or a cookie made with chickpea, coconut, or almond flour will do just fine.

Keeping a Lid on the Cauldron

Imagine cooking rice in a pot. Once you put the lid on and turn the heat down, you must keep it covered in order for the steam to be properly absorbed. Otherwise, the pressure and moisture are released and the rice doesn't plump up as it should.

Similarly, your spells, rituals, and all magical efforts to create positive change in your life must be properly contained in order to manifest in a desirable way. After you add in the rice and cover the pot, don't open the lid over and over again and say, "Look, everyone! I'm cooking rice!" In other words, don't go around telling everyone, "I just did a spell to manifest a new job!" It's fine if those closest to you know you're *looking* for a job, but by all means, keep a lid on your magical work. By doing so, you protect the precious energetic conditions you've created from the opinions, expectations, and thought currents of others. You allow the magic to unfold without extra pressure from outside observation. In short, you preserve the conditions necessary for success.

Another aspect of keeping a lid on the cauldron is trusting the ideal conditions to unfold. If you keep opening the lid to make sure the rice is cooking properly, it won't. Similarly, if you do a money spell and then worry endlessly about just how exactly the money is going to arrive, you're not allowing the universe to do its thing.

If it feels difficult to release the conditions and trust the universe, you can quiet your thoughts and circumvent the tendency to hold on or micromanage by repeating this affirmation silently or aloud, for as long as necessary:

Infinite power goes before me, easily orchestrating perfect success.

····················· YOUR MAGIC ·····················
Cast a Self-Initiation Spell
*There are so many reasons that people assume that they
can never become a magician, witch, wizard, warlock, practitioner,
adept, whatever word you prefer. … That's all old baggage. Throw it
away. None of it prevents you from achieving your full potential now.*
~ JUDIKA ILLES, *THE BIG BOOK OF PRACTICAL SPELLS*

The power of an initiation spell is that it sends a clear message to the totality of you—i.e., your mind, body, spirit, and the part of you that is one with All That Is—that you have chosen to commit to your magical path: to consciously work with the natural and invisible powers at work in order to create positive change according to your will. This boosts your focus, rallies your unseen allies, and amplifies your magical power.

And if you've really and truly read every chapter up to this point and faithfully performed all the integration exercises, then I hereby pronounce you ready to do a spell to initiate yourself into your craft.

I mean, if you'd like to. Would you? If so, here's what you'll do. First, gather these ingredients:

- A clear quartz crystal point, cleansed with bright sunlight for two to five minutes
- A pentacle pendant that you like (Don't worry, you won't have to wear it all the time, unless you want to.)
- The fresh petals from one white rose, spread out on a dinner plate

Next, choose an initiation patron. This could be a god or goddess from any pantheon, a saint, a totem or spirit animal, an archangel, a deceased loved one who you feel supports your path, or any other beneficent being in the unseen world that feels right to you.

With your ingredients nearby, call the quarters and cast a circle as outlined in this chapter. Don't worry about doing it perfectly. Just do your best.

While facing east, call on your initiation patron by saying something like this:

[Name of patron], I call on you. I ask you to bless my magical spiritual path.

I promise to do my best to align my will with divine will, to honor nature in all ways, and to boldly create the life conditions I desire.

I promise to do my best to harm none and to act in the interest of the highest and truest good of all.

Place the crystal and pendant on top of the rose petals on the plate. Hold the plate on both hands. Say:

With perfect love, perfect trust,
Clear and focused intention,
And a deep reverence and respect for the interconnectedness of all,
I commit myself to a life of magic and I step into my magical power.

Feel and sense pure white light shining down upon you, filling your aura, blessing your intention, and illuminating the crystal and pendant with powerful magical energy. Do your best to feel this light pulsating within and around you.

When it feels right, place the plate on the floor. Hang the pendant around your neck and hold the crystal in your right hand. With your left hand, scatter the petals around the inside of the circle. With great reverence and gratitude, say:

It is done.

While still holding the crystal and wearing the pendant, thank the quarters, open the circle, and earth the power as outlined earlier. Again, don't worry about doing it perfectly. Just do your best.

In the future, you can use the crystal as a magical tool to help you focus your power and intention. For example, you could use it in lieu of your right finger when casting a circle, or place it on top of a written intention on your altar. When you're not using it, you might keep it on a sunny windowsill to keep its energy clear and bright.

The pendant can be worn during ritual and any other time you'd like an extra dose of power and protection.

9

Living Magically Every Day

You're magical every moment of every day. It's not just an identity you assume when you're reading the cards or casting a spell. You're crafting your reality constantly. Your words are powerful. Your thoughts are powerful. Even what you have for breakfast is powerful.

Of course, while this demands that you live presently, consciously, and purposefully, it doesn't mean you need to freak out about every little thing. Quite the contrary! It means it's ideal to feel as much confidence and flow as possible, as often as possible. This calls for both noticing negative thoughts *and* forgiving yourself for them. It calls for honestly admitting where you'd like things to be different, and also blessing them just as they are. *And* it calls for sustainable, reliable, empowering methods of living magically every day.

Will you always follow the guidelines in this chapter to the letter, and will that in turn make you an eternally perfect magic worker and problem-free person? Not a chance in Hogwarts, Hermione! But you will have a lifetime to practice navigating the ups and downs of this human experience, and you will gain in wisdom with every challenge and mistake. All the while, you'll spiral deeper and deeper into the heart of self-mastery and authentic magical power.

That way, while every day you may lose a bit more of your youth, you'll gain a bit more of your eternal, Goddess-given radiance. So while everyone else is worried about staying young, you'll be gazing unflinchingly in the mirror, admiring the ever-more luminous twinkle in your eye.

Sacred Space

As a magical person, you know that the entire earth is sacred, and you are a channel of divine wisdom and power. This means your home is holy ground. When someone walks into your home, if they are the least bit sensitive to energy, you want them to feel that they are entering a sacred space. We want you to feel that same way.

As we've seen, your feelings are powerful, and like attracts like. So when you look around your home and love it, your entire life benefits. You feel lucky and rich, so you draw more luck and riches. You feel loved and lovable, so you draw more love into your life. You feel like your life is a triumph, so you draw ever-expanding success.

As you may know, I've written entire books and scores of blog posts on creating sacred space. That's why I'm uniquely qualified to boil it down for you into these key points.

Clear your clutter. If you get rid of all the extras from everywhere, you'll free up a ton of stuck energy. You'll also create the space for way more blessings to flow into your life experience.

Clean. Cleaning has a reputation for being the most mundane of mundane activities, but actually it's one of the most magical things you can do. Cleaning improves the vibration of your home, which improves your personal vibration, which instantly magnetizes beautiful and harmonious life conditions. Knowing this, you can treat it like the magical act it is and have way more fun with it than you otherwise would. Put on some music you love, wear something beautiful, burn some incense, and choose natural and holistic cleaning products that smell divine.

Clear the energy. We touched on this in chapter 6, but it's worth revisiting. Clearing the energy is a way of cleaning the invisible aspect of your home: getting stuck energy moving and transmuting negativity into positivity and flow. A bundle of dried white sage is the go-to clearing tool for many, and is in fact all you really need. It erases negativity like a delete button. You can make your own (by bundling up a bunch of fresh white sage with hemp twine and then drying it) or purchase a sage bundle at most metaphysical supply stores. When you're ready to clear, open all the windows. Light the sage so it's burning like incense, carry a dish or plate under it to catch any burning embers, and move around each room and area in a counterclockwise direction, wafting the smoke all around as you go. Then extinguish it by sealing it in a jar or running it under water.

Alternatively, many people prefer palo santo wood, frankincense incense, or desert sage, all of which work similarly.

Or, if you have asthma, your smoke alarm is on a hair trigger, or you just don't like the smell of burning plants, you can use a smudge spray. For example, I like the Sacred Smudge Spray at eyeofhorus.biz. As mentioned in chapter 6, you can also create your own smudge spray by adding ten to twenty drops of essential oil (such as sage, clary sage, cedar, and/or lavender) to a mister of spring water.

Cover your television. Can you imagine walking into the living room in the house from the film *Practical Magic* and seeing a giant television screen? Never! Seriously, if you have a television, be a self-respecting magical person and cover that thing with an attractive cloth or tapestry when you're not watching it. You could also obtain a piece of furniture created specifically for the purpose of television concealment.

Keep your toilet lid closed. Now that you're becoming more and more sensitive to energy, can you feel how an uncovered toilet sort of drains all the buoyant energy out of the room? Luckily, covering it between uses (with the lid that it so conveniently comes with) fixes that problem.

Decorate like you're adorning a temple. From a magical perspective, every second of every day is sacred, and this entire life experience is an opportunity to commune with earthly wisdom and celestial power. Sure, we might forget that sometimes, but you know what helps us remember? Decorating our home like a temple: choosing colors, patterns, fabrics, furniture, and imagery that remind us of our divine nature and the divinity that abides within all things. This doesn't mean you have to spend a bunch of money, though. Utter simplicity with a few divine flourishes (such as prayer flags, African violets, and some naturally scented candles) can be just as sacred as anything.

Make it smell good. For so many of us, walking into a New Age bookstore elevates our consciousness instantly, mostly because it smells like heaven. That's why I highly recommend making your home smell like that by burning incense regularly. My favorite brand is Fred Soll's Resin on a Stick, but I like lots of other ones too, and I'm sure you'll find your own favorites (or make your own if you're crafty like that). Additionally (or instead, if you're not a smoke person), you can burn a lot of naturally scented soy candles and diffuse a lot of essential oils. I like to burn incense on my altars every morning and/or evening, as offerings to the representations of the Divine featured on them. (This has the added benefit of calling their unique energetic presence into my home.)

Enchanted Eating

I'll say it again: everything is energy. Our vibration attracts what we experience. And what could have a greater effect on our personal vibration than the vibrations we ingest through our food? I'm not saying you can't work successful magic after eating cheese puffs and powdered donuts, but I *am* saying it won't be easy. Plus, you won't feel so great. And how we feel defines our reality and magnetizes our life conditions. So obviously, feeling great is pretty important.

Of course, no two magic workers are alike, so you'll want to find an eating strategy that works for you. Still, there are some universally helpful tips when it comes to eating a high-vibrational, magic-friendly diet.

Bless your food and beverages before you eat and drink them.
No matter what you eat or drink, it's a great idea to bless it first. To do so, hold the food or beverage in both hands or simply hold your hands in prayer pose over it. Close your eyes (or keep them open if you want to be discreet) and call on the Divine in a way that feels powerful for you. Then envision golden-white light filling and surrounding the food or drink, attuning it with

your body and with the clearest and most positive vibrations possible. Feel deep gratitude for your food and for the divine energy that blesses it.

Drink lots of water. Drinking lots and lots of clear, pure water throughout the day is a must for both physical and energetic bodies. In addition to the countless physical benefits we always hear about, water helps keep your intuition clear and your aura bright (especially when you bless it first!).

Lean toward whole food in general. If you're going to eat grains, eat whole grains. If you're going to eat fruit, eat whole fruit (not fruit juice, which is very close to sugar). This way, you'll get the full, natural nutritional benefits as well as the vibrant life force energy associated with the plant. Eating lots of whole fruits and vegetables, especially, will bless your aura with a robust vibration that is largely immune to all forms of negativity. (I personally don't eat animal products, as I find my body, mind, and spirit work much better without them, but if you do, it would be wise to do so in the healthiest, kindest, and most reverent way possible.)

Go really easy on sugary, packaged, and processed foods, or cut them out altogether. If your energy field is like a pristine forest, then eating sugary, processed, or packaged foods is like throwing potato chip bags and beer cans all over the forest floor, not to mention the strain it puts on your liver to clear out those toxic foreign substances. On the other hand, eating nothing but whole, natural foods helps your magic stay powerful, positive, and pure.

Consider cutting out dairy, or going really light on it. Very few people can actually digest dairy, and when you get sick, the dairy in your system actually keeps you sick longer. Ever get those coughs or colds that hang on and on and then keep coming back? Dairy increases your body's mucus production. Try cutting it out of your diet *completely* for at least a month, and when colds do show up, they'll go away within days or may not even show up in the first place. (I know it's a bold claim. If you don't believe me, try it and see.)

Go light on the booze. Of course, magic workers are fae creatures. In other words, we're wild. Many of us like to party now and then, and perhaps to have a bit of beer or ale after casting a spell. And there's nothing wrong with that! But the fact is, regular over-drinking taxes your liver, muddies up your intuition, and gives your aura a dingy cast.* It can also attract less-than-savory entities that hang out in your energy field, which is especially dangerous when you're doing what magic workers do: consciously working between the worlds of form and spirit. So party once in a while—fine! Even get rip-roaring drunk a few times a year. But regular drinking is a bad idea for everyone, especially those of us on the magical path.

* The same is true of regular drug use. While some herbal hallucinogens and marijuana can be used for spiritual purposes without any adverse effects on your energy field, it's still important to use them consciously and in moderation.

Physical Fitness

Your body is literally electric. When you exercise regularly, you charge up your body's electrical emanation, giving your aura a strong, constant glow of protective strength and positivity. So find something you love to do, and when you get tired of it, find something else! Simply jumping on a treadmill and frequenting the weight room would be great, but if you'd like, you can pair your physical fitness with something that noticeably aligns you with Spirit, such as sacred dance, yoga, surfing, hiking, or tai chi. Incidentally, all these activities can become magical acts in themselves. For example, you can dance for joy, do yoga for world peace, lift weights to get stuck energy moving, surf to cleanse your chakras, hike up a mountain to open up to inspiration, or do tai chi to heal your mind, body, and spirit.

The Akashic Records

Many magical folk, including me, believe in past lives, and believe our past lives influence our current life in very real ways. (If you don't believe in past lives, I urge you to read the book *Old Souls* by Tom Shroder. At the very least, it will give you some facts to consider.) As such, we can create positive change in our lives through influencing our present relationship with our past lives, as well as with past traumas in this life, by accessing an information-rich field of energy called the *akashic records*.

When you have a solid understanding of what the akashic records are, how they work, and how you can influence them, you step into a much greater level of mastery of your magic and your entire life experience.

According to Ervin László in his book *Science and the Akashic Field,*

> Akasha … is a Sanskrit word meaning "ether": all-pervasive space. Originally signifying "radiation" or "brilliance," … Akasha embraces the properties of all five elements: it is the womb from which everything we perceive with our senses has emerged and into which everything will ultimately redescend. "The Akashic Record" … is the enduring record of

all that happens, and has ever happened, in the whole of the universe.

There is one giant akashic record, and then there is your personal file within the larger whole: your own akashic record. This is the underlying field of energy and information that informs and defines your life experience. You might think of it as the code that underwrites the program that is you. It includes all traumas, beliefs, vows, and patterns from this life and all other lives, in all directions of time, and on all planes and levels of reality. Some of these patterns may have been worn away and broken down, similar to how rocks turn to sand after centuries of being washed up on the shore. Other patterns may stick around, secretly lurking beneath your conscious awareness, causing you to be in a sort of loop where you experience the same challenge or limitation over and over and over again.

Why do some patterns stick around while others get worn away? Because your soul wants to learn something specific before you move on from each pattern. It wants to be initiated into a certain type of wisdom and to experience a certain type of blessing you couldn't experience any other way. Once you learn the lesson hidden within the challenge, the pattern will break down and the soul's desired blessing will emerge.

A great way to start working with the akashic records is to engage in a past-life regression meditation. This will allow you to visit the source of a recurring challenge that's been holding you back.

You needn't spend a bunch of money on a professional past-life regression, unless you want to. Personally, I've had startling success with self-guided meditations such as the following one.

·············· YOUR MAGIC ·····················

Discover a Past Life

Find somewhere quiet and relaxing where you won't be disturbed. Lie flat on your back in a comfortable way, propping up your head and/or knees as necessary.

Before beginning the meditation, set the intention to reconnect with a past life that will shed light on a challenge from this present life. Further intend to heal the challenge by bathing the memory of the trauma in the light of awareness and compassion.

Inhale deeply, hold your breath for a second, and tense up everything in your body as tightly as you safely can. Exhale fully as you release all tension along with the breath. Repeat three times. Then allow your breathing to be natural as you continue to release any remaining tension and relax as deeply as possible.

Imagine you are asleep and dreaming of a magic carpet ride. See and sense yourself zooming high above the earth in this dream realm, looking down at the earth below. Notice that the landscape is changing as you go back in time in your dream. Go back, go back, go back, go back. Then, in your mind's eye, awaken. And through the lens of your imagining mind, explore the place where you happen to be.

Are you in a bed? Are you on the ground? Where are you?

Sit up, stretch, and stand up. What are you wearing?

Look around the room or area. What does it look like?

How old are you? Are you male or female?

Is there someone else nearby, or are you alone?

Now go to a significant moment in this life experience. What is happening? What are you saying? What are you doing? How do you feel?

Now go to another significant moment. What's happening now? What are you saying? What are you doing? How do you feel?

Fast-forward now to your transition out of this life. Where are you? What are the details of what we call your "death" in this life?

Allow yourself to pass out of that life by having the experience we call "death," but notice that it isn't much different than going to sleep.

Enter into the realm of light and connection where you know for certain that you are safe, you are loved, and you are one with everything. Allow yourself to heal fully and completely from the traumas in that lifetime and the related ones in this present lifetime.

Choose to return to this present life. Enter a tunnel of light on your magic carpet and return to your present body. Inhabit it now. Feel yourself in the room. Wiggle your fingers and toes. Open your eyes.

In a journal, write what you experienced. How did the past life relate to your current life? What challenges seem related? Now that you have a longer view and an enhanced perspective, what wisdom and insight have you gained? How can you approach the challenges differently? How can you evolve?

This is something you can revisit when you notice a challenging pattern or limitation (such as a relationship issue or a block to financial abundance) that keeps showing up again and again.

Finding Your People

I may have never met you personally, but because you've read this far in the book, I know some stuff about you. For example, I know magic is an integral part of your identity. Even if you're just learning about it on a conscious level, it's something you've sensed beneath your conscious awareness for a long time. Now that you're learning about it, it's as if you've discovered a whole new language that allows you to communicate on many more levels, and in much more dimensional detail, than ever before. So obviously, you're going to want to find your people with whom you can communicate: to assemble a community (even a very tiny one) of other dear, exquisite, and sensitive creatures who speak the language of magic.

Don't worry, you don't have to endure any cultish weirdness, go through an elaborate coven initiation, or try to fit in with the cool kids. In fact, if you're like me, you'll prefer to make a few friends who think like you do and then get together every now and then to celebrate pagan holidays, talk about your spirit guides, reminisce about your past lives, watch a campy witch movie or two, or just generally geek out on magic for hours on end. Let it be natural: there's no rush and there's no need to make it official. Start by setting the intention to magnetize a magical group of friends, and then joyfully expect it to happen easily and in divine timing.

But where will you meet these folks? You never know—you could meet them anywhere. But you'll up your chances if you attend things like these:

- Spiritual classes and workshops at a local metaphysical center or store
- A pagan gathering in or near your state
- A Pagan Pride Day in a nearby urban area

You can also find a magical community online and then find out if any members of the group live in your area. I happen to be partial to the Good Vibe Tribe, which is the magical community I facilitate, but there are of course plenty to choose from.

························ YOUR MAGIC ·······················

Plan a Month of Everyday Magical Living

Tell me, what is it you plan to do with your one wild and precious life?
~ MARY OLIVER, "THE SUMMER DAY"

It may not be New Year's Day, but it's a personal new beginning: you're embarking on a lifetime of magical work. So go back through this chapter and make a list of your goals for living the magical life every day. Then plan out one month by adding your goals to your calendar. (You might want to get a brand-new planner that has the space to accommodate your spiritual and magical activities right along with your everyday ones.)

For example, week one (which could start tomorrow, next Monday, at the next new moon, or really whenever feels right) might include thirty minutes of clutter clearing, ten minutes of meditation, and thirty minutes of exercise every day.

Week two might include a trip to the grocery store with the intention to switch to a clean diet, some time for creating sacred space in your home, and of course daily meditation and almost daily exercise.

Week three might feature a tarot workshop you found out about at your local metaphysical bookstore, a past-life regression meditation, continued clean eating, daily meditation, and almost daily exercise.

Week four could again feature thirty minutes of clutter clearing per day, during which you delve even more deeply into the practice than you did in week one. (For example, you could clear out your glove compartment, roll up loose change, and delete old down-loads from your computer.) You could also add some flourishes to your sacred space, such as altar offerings and fresh flowers, and of course continue the regular meditation and exercise.

For the final couple of days in the month, you might do a deep space-clearing ritual and then perform a spell to manifest one of your heart's fondest desires. (If you're looking for spell ideas, the second half of this book is full of them!)

As the month draws to a close, you can plan for another magical month or just naturally stay in the groove of living magically every day.

Part 2

• • •

*Working Your
Magic*

10

Manifesting Abundance

It is natural for you to be constantly flowing with prosperous blessings, like those found in nature. Where I live, an abundance of rain and snow falls every autumn and winter, bringing forth a wealth of aspen leaves, dandelions, bluebells, wild roses, blackberries, and blades of grass in the spring. As the stockpile of snow melts in the highest elevations, a seemingly endless deluge of pure water flows generously and melodically through the many mountain streams as blindingly bright sunlight sparkles on its surface like so many golden coins.

The spells in this section are designed to help you tap into your natural flow of abundance, so that your life is filled with ease, contentment, luxury, and ever-increasing riches.

Please note that you can vastly increase the effectiveness of all of these spells by thoroughly clearing clutter and cleaning house before you begin. This works on the principle that nature abhors a vacuum. By getting rid of what you *don't* want, you create space for what you *do* want. It also creates the type of energy that wealth loves. In India, it is said that Lakshmi, the goddess of prosperity, won't enter a messy or dirty home.

Clear Blocks to Prosperity

Do you have the sense that you're holding yourself back from receiving the abundant blessings the universe so dearly desires to bestow upon you? This spell will help you clear blocks to wealth, such as negative beliefs, limiting family paradigms, paralyzing fears, past-life patterns, and internalized cultural messages.

Ingredients
A white candle and holder
¼ cup sea salt
A grapefruit, cut into eight pieces

On the full moon or when the moon is waning, draw a bath. Light the candle and turn out any electric lights. Add the salt and grapefruit to the bath water and stir with your left hand in a counterclockwise direction for eight total rotations. Get into the water. Recline, relax deeply, and center yourself as you take some calming breaths. When you feel ready, with great authority, say:

Glorious Goddess, God beloved,
Earth below and sky above,
Assist me now as I release
All blocks to money, joy, and peace.
I choose now to clearly see
That you adore and treasure me.
You love to share your gifts divine
Of sustenance and luxuries fine.
Old vows now break, old patterns shift,
As I with joy accept your gifts.
With gratitude and love for thee,
As I will it, so mote it be.

(It's okay to have the chant written down to read while you soak.)

Continue to soak for around ten to twenty minutes, feeling your energy field receive an upgrade as all old blocks to financial abundance fall away. Afterward, compost the grapefruit slices or place them on the earth to naturally biodegrade.

Expand Your Capacity for Wealth

We all have a preprogrammed set point for how much wealth we are prepared to receive, based on past-life experiences, family patterns, cultural programming, habit, and personal beliefs. That's why so many lottery winners quickly find themselves at pretty much precisely the level of financial abundance they were experiencing before they won. But we can work magic to raise this set point, and we can do so throughout our lifetime! While we might expand our capacity for wealth at intervals (like digging a ditch deeper and deeper to allow more and more water to flow through it over time), there is ultimately no limit to how much we can allow ourselves to accept and receive.

This ritual will help you expand your capacity to receive wealth, and thereby increase your natural flow of abundance.

Ingredients

A flower of life crystal grid cloth, around 12–18 inches by 12–18 inches (This is a cloth depicting the sacred geometry mandala called the *flower of life*. You can find one on Etsy.com and at some metaphysical supply stores, or make your own if you're crafty like that.)

A stick or cone of sage incense and holder

Your full name, written on a small round or radial-shaped piece of paper

8 aventurine stones, cleansed in sunlight for 2–5 minutes

8 shiny quarters, washed in salt water

Fresh rose petals of any color (optional)

On a Thursday or a Sunday when the moon is waxing, play an up-lifting piece of classical music that you like. Spread the cloth on a table and light the incense nearby. Center yourself as you take some deep breaths and come fully into the moment. Clearly and decisively set your intention by saying simply and with great power:

> *I now connect with my infinite self and thank God/Goddess/*
> *All That Is for assisting me in opening up to a generous, endless,*
> *ever-expanding flow of wealth.*

Hold the paper with your name written on it over the incense, bathing it in the smoke. Place it in the center of the flower of life mandala. Now take some time to arrange the aventurine stones and quarters around your name in a way that feels right, being sure to bathe each one in the incense smoke before you place it on the cloth. (It's okay to rearrange them after you've placed each one initially.) If you're working with rose petals as well, arrange them artfully around the outside of the mandala.

When it looks just the way you want it to, admire the beauty of what you've created as you feel joy and gratitude in your heart. Feel, sense, and know that your capacity for wealth is greatly expanding. Feel even more gratitude. Then say:

> *Thank you, thank you, thank you.*
> *Blessed be. And so it is.*

Leave the mandala artwork for at least twenty-four hours and up to fourteen days. Give the quarters away to a good cause, keep the aventurines and flower of life cloth for future magical use, recycle the paper, and scatter any rose petals outside where they can naturally biodegrade.

Transform Yourself into a Rich(er) Person

Financial abundance is relative. For example, most of us in the Western world are currently enjoying far more luxuries than the most pampered royals of eons past, who often had no running water, no central heat, few books, lots of fleas, and truly deplorable health care options. On the other hand, the spectrum of financial abundance is vast. In other words, we pretty much always have room to transform ourselves into an even richer person than we already are. This spell will help you do that.

Ingredients

A brand-new doormat that you love and that you imagine a rich(er) person would own (Take your time to find the right one.)

A shiny silver dollar

A pinch of saffron

Essential oil of cinnamon and a small paintbrush (optional)

While the moon is waxing, remove your old doormat (if you have one) and thoroughly sweep your doorstep. Place your new doormat in front of your door. Place the silver dollar under it. Lightly crush the saffron between your fingers and scatter it under the doormat as well. Optionally, use the paintbrush to lightly brush a tiny bit of cinnamon oil on the front door. (Be careful not to let the oil touch your skin, as it can be irritating.) Say:

> By sun and moon, by earth and sky,
> This home's rich resident is I!

Feel free to refresh the magic sometimes if you'd like. Do so by sweeping under and around the doormat, replacing the silver dollar, replacing the saffron (and optionally the cinnamon oil), and repeating the chant. Just keep it to no more than once per moon cycle.

Donate or discard your old doormat as appropriate.

Manifest a Particular Amount of Money

When there's a certain amount of money that you'd like to conjure up, try this spell. You can do it for fun (to practice your manifestation skills and magnetize a bit of wealth in the process) or for a particular purpose (such as buying a car or treating yourself to a vacation).

Ingredients

Sunflower oil

A dollar bill

A clear quartz crystal point, cleansed in bright sunlight for 2–5 minutes

A spool of extra-sturdy bright red thread

Do this spell on a Tuesday, Thursday, or Sunday when the moon is waxing and in a fire sign (i.e., Aries, Leo, or Sagittarius). With the sunflower oil, use your finger to trace the amount of money you'd like to manifest on the dollar bill. Then spread the bill out flat between your two palms and rub your palms together, imagining the wealth you seek being irresistibly magnetized to the warmth and energy generated by this movement. As you do this, say:

$_____, wherever you are,
Come to me from near or far.
$_____ that I seek,

Come to me within three weeks.
I bid you now by fire and sun
To multiply to $_____ times one.

Fold the dollar bill longways once or twice (folding toward you each time), and then wrap the quartz crystal in it like a burrito (again rolling toward you). Tightly tie it with the thread. Place it on your altar until the money arrives.

When the charm has served its purpose, untie it. Dispose of the thread, give the dollar bill away to a person or cause, and keep the quartz for future magical use.

Call In a Constant Flow of Financial Abundance

The Hindu goddess Lakshmi bestows blessings of wealth, abundance, luxury, beauty, and love. She is most fond of doing so when we revere her regularly. And we're talking, like, every day—not just once in a while. That's why this spell is more like a lifestyle choice than a one-time event. So don't commit to it lightly. (Optionally, you can adapt this altar spell to honor an abundance deity of your preference.)

Ingredients

A pink or violet altar cloth

A statue of Lakshmi that you love

A generous supply of violet-colored votive candles (replenished as needed)

A votive candle holder

A generous supply of rose and/or Nag Champa incense (replenished as needed)

An incense holder

A small vase and a constantly replenished fresh flower or two (optional)

On a Thursday when the moon is waxing, create an altar to Lakshmi (or the abundance deity of your choice). Start by spreading the altar cloth on a small table or other flat surface. (Note that this altar will be a permanent design feature of your home from now on.) On the cloth, place the statue, votive holder with candle, incense holder with a stick of incense, and optional vase with flower. Light the candle. Light the incense and take a moment to waft it around the statue while inwardly chanting Lakshmi's seed sound* over and over:

Shrim, shrim, shrim, shrim, shrim…

Then put the incense back in the holder. Allow the candle and incense to burn for at least ten minutes. Repeat once daily, five to seven times per week. (Don't worry if you go on vacation or something. Just keep up with it when you're home.)

* A seed sound, also known as a *bija mantra*, is a spoken sound with no literal translation that possesses a powerful, transformational vibration.

11

Activating Success

Respect and recognition are like fire. You can stoke that fire in order to transform glowing coals of potential into a raging, ever-expanding inferno.

On the other hand, the individual expression of your ideal life path is like water. You can clear the way for it to flow with ever-increasing authenticity, momentum, and depth until it recognizes itself as the deep, abiding depths of the sea.

Recognition without life path alignment burns us out. Life path alignment without recognition strands us all alone in the swamp. But when the two balance each other, you are truly a success: your life is filled with nourishment, inspiration, and satisfying self-expression. Your radiance is like the sun, shining on the cool, deep waters of your life path. You offer the world wonderful things, and the world offers you a generous flow of wealth in return.

These spells are designed to help you dial in to the marvelous alchemy of true success.

Amplify Everyday Magnetism

Some people have that indefinable quality that has come to be known as *it*. Doors of opportunity magically appear for them as if out of thin air. People meet them and instantly want to hire them (or work for them or marry them). A trail of magical coincidences seems to follow in their wake. They don't have to do a lot of chasing after things because positive life conditions seem to be chasing after *them*. Why resent these people, or simply admire them from afar, when you can join their ranks? That's what this spell is for.

Ingredients

Gold gem essence (available at AlaskanEssences.com)

A clean wine glass or chalice of fresh drinking water

A fresh wisteria or lilac blossom, lovingly gathered or obtained (You can substitute a white or violet-colored rose if wisteria and lilac are both unavailable.)

A necklace you like featuring a pendant in the shape of a triangle (any material)

Place four drops of the gem essence in the water. Swish it around. Visualize golden-white light with sparkles filling and surrounding the water as you say:

Water of gold, awaken my radiance, activate my light.

Drink the entire glass of water, feeling the golden-white light filling and illuminating you.

Hold the flower in your right hand. Visualize it illuminated with violet light as you say:

Beguiling blossom, activate and magnify my ability to easily attract all that is beautiful and good.

Brush your entire aura with the flower, about six to twelve inches away from your skin. (Imagine you are using a lint brush on your aura as you lightly brush down and away.) Then touch the flower to the center of your forehead, your throat, your heart, and your belly.

Pick up the pendant and hold it in your left hand. Touch it with the flower and say:

I am naturally magnetic to all forms of success and wealth. I am lucky beyond my fondest dreams. All of heaven and earth now conspire to bless me with every wonderful thing.

Hang the pendant around your neck. Wear it whenever you'd like to turn up the volume on your radiance, charisma, and everyday magnetism.

After the spell, gratefully return the flower to the earth by placing it near the base of a tree.

Ignite Your Fame

Even if you don't want to be a movie star, you do want to be seen, known, and appreciated for the skills, qualities, and accomplishments that make you proud. I know this because you're a human! We all want to be recognized in this way. It's universal.

This spell will help you ignite the radiant emanation of you, so that you're on fire in the most wonderful of ways, for all the world to see.

Ingredients

A fire, safely burning in a fireplace or fire pit

Paper and pen

9 small dried pine or eucalyptus twigs

Relax and center yourself while gazing into the fire. When you feel ready, write your full name and full birth date in the center of the paper. Surrounding it, write everything you'd like to be seen, known, and appreciated for. For example, you could write qualities, activities, skills, the name of your business or occupation, the products you produce, and/or any other words or phrases that you'd like to characterize your unique brand of fame, such as "Everyone's favorite," "Authentically excellent," and "The BEST!" When it feels complete, throw the paper on the fire. Make sure to do so in such a way that it will burn completely. You may need to crumple it a bit to be sure.

As the paper burns, throw the nine twigs on the fire as well. Then say:

> *With this raging, gorgeous flame,*
> *I now ignite my perfect fame.*

After the spell, be sure to follow commonsense fire safety guidelines as you usually would but with an extra helping of caution, considering the fire magic you just invoked.

Lock Into Your Life Path

Life path is another way of saying *career path* but in a more spiritual sense. *Career* has the connotation of being mainly finance-driven. While you may indeed make a fortune from aligning with your life path, it's about much more than that: it's about being your authentic self, doing the things that inspire you and bring you joy, and sharing those gifts with the world.

For example, your divine life path might largely involve pursuits not known for their money-making potential, such as parenting or gardening or volunteering at your local animal shelter. Although who knows? You might write a popular blog on one of these topics or be a sought-after speaker on the subject. The point is money may be involved, but it's not the point.

Your life path is already in full swing—you just may not know it yet. Every experience you have, every skill you learn, and even every "mistake" you make is a step along the path of fulfilling the mission your soul is choosing to accomplish in this lifetime. Still, you can work magic to lock into your life path in a way that feels conscious, purposeful, and satisfying. Even then, you may not see the whole path (in fact, you almost certainly won't), but you'll see the next step and you'll feel joy and a sense of expansion when you take it. Then you'll see the next step and the next.

This spell will help you connect with your life path: to lock into a satisfying sense of purpose and flow.

Ingredients

A moonstone (a simple crystal or a piece of jewelry that you love)
A small notebook and a pen (Maybe splurge and get a notebook and pen you especially love.)

When the moon is new, cleanse the moonstone in bright sunlight or sage smoke. With ingredients in tow, visit a natural body of water. Sit or stand comfortably in front of it, gazing at it as you take some deep breaths, relax your body, and center your mind.

When you feel centered, begin to mentally and energetically align your being with the water. Feel that you *are* the water. Imagine that you are fluid, and that you allow yourself to flow and inhabit your life in a way that is natural to you.

Next, take the moonstone to the water and dunk it in. Hold it under for a moment to attune it to the water's frequency. When it's still wet, lightly touch it to your forehead, heart, and belly. Then wear it or put it in your pocket, and keep it with you for at least the next twenty-eight days (one full moon cycle).

Also set the intention to keep the notebook and pen with you at all times (even keeping it next to you while you sleep) for the next twenty-eight days. During that time, record anything that ignites your sense of inspiration, joy, excitement, or expansiveness. It could be a phrase, an activity, a possibility, a country, a tradition, or something beautiful you experience, such as a hummingbird, the sound of wind chimes, or the scent of pavement after it rains.

Return to the natural body of water at the following new moon, again with your notebook, pen, and moonstone. Sit comfortably and center yourself. Align with the water. Then take some time to look through your notes. Do so like a detective: What patterns do you recognize? How might these things fit together? What do they have in common? Whether or not you find answers to these questions, you will indeed be able to answer this one: What one step in life feels the most exciting and expansive to you now? It may or may not seem to be career-related. For example, it could be moving to a new city or starting a brand-new health and fitness regimen. It could also be embarking on a course of study, setting up a personal practice of some sort, or kicking off your artistic career. Whatever it is, it will probably feel both thrilling and terrifying. Trust that you know what it is. (If you think you don't, ask yourself: If I did, what would it be?) Write it down. Then over the course of the next moon cycle, create a definitive plan for doing it, and put it into action.

Until you feel really and truly locked into your life path, you can continue to keep your moonstone with you and/or place it prominently on your altar.

Boost Your Harmony in the Workplace

When I was fairly new to the magical path, I did a spell to protect myself from the negative vibes emanating from my boss. The very next day, she fired me—seemingly out of the blue! In fact, she had just given me a raise the previous week. Clearly, the particular type of harmony I was seeking just wasn't possible with that particular job. The good news was that I found a new position within days, and my new boss was as friendly and supportive as could be.

The moral of the story is that you can always create harmony. But considering that the free will of others is involved, that harmony might not look the way you thought it would.

That being said, this charm will help shield you from negativity, establish and preserve your inner equilibrium, and generally boost your personal harmony quotient at work.

Ingredient

An amethyst spirit quartz pendant necklace that rests over your heart area, cleansed in bright sunlight

Cradle the necklace in your left palm. Cup your right palm over your left. Feel your right hand emanating energy and light as you say:

My heart is calm, my joy is bright,
I'm safe within a sphere of light.

Wear the pendant every day for protection and peace. At least once per moon cycle, cleanse the pendant in sunlight and repeat the chanting process to keep the magic strong.

Supercharge Your Career

When you love your career and it truly feels authentic to you and your talents, you have the prerequisites in place for both abiding excellence and stellar success. This ritual will activate both these qualities.

Ingredients
A dark blue or purple candle and holder
A piece of paper and a pen
A half-pint Mason jar with a lid
9 dried pansy blossoms
Dragon's blood powder (This is an incense resin, available online and at many metaphysical supply stores.)

Between 11:30 p.m. and 12:30 a.m. on the night of a full moon, light the candle. On the paper, write the following sentences, filling in the blanks according to what you are choosing to manifest. Be sure to write all sentences in the present tense, as if they are already true.

I love my career.
It fulfills my heart's desire to _____.
I love it because I help others to _____.
I love it because I get to express my natural talents of _____,
_____, and _____.
I love it because I spread the positive qualities of _____.
I make $_____ per _____ or more.

Include any other qualities you'd like to experience in your career. Remember, write everything in the present tense! Then write:

Thank you, thank you, thank you.
Blessed be. And so it is.

At the bottom, sign your name and add the date.

With great conviction and joy, read aloud what you have written on the paper. Fold it up so it will fit in the jar, being sure to fold it toward you each time.

Place it in the jar. Put the pansy blossoms on top and sprinkle a pinch or two of dragon's blood powder on top. Close the jar and place it on your altar. Keep it there until the next full moon. Then, during the waning moon cycle, release the dragon's blood and pansies into a moving body of water. Safely burn the paper in a cauldron, fireplace, or fire pit. Wash the jar and save it for future use.

Bless a Business or Job

Whether it's a day job to pay the bills, a career position you'd like to keep for the long haul, a business you've inherited, or a business you've purchased or started yourself, you may as well magically drench it in abundant blessings of sweetness, beauty, and success.

Ingredients

A business card (You can create one just for the purpose of this spell if you don't already have some made.)

A pen

A small, pretty glass bottle with a cork stopper (Check World Market or another import shop.)

Cinnamon

Dried rose petals

Maple syrup

Do this spell during a waxing moon on a Tuesday, Thursday, or Sunday.

Over the top of whatever is written on the front of your business card, write *Success!* three times. Then roll up the business card (rolling it toward you) and place it in the bottle. Sprinkle it with cinnamon and dried rose petals while repeating the word *success!* Continue chanting as you cover everything in the bottle with maple syrup, filling it to the top. Close the bottle with the cork.

With a wet sponge or cloth, wipe off any sticky maple syrup on the outside of the bottle. Place it on your altar for at least one full moon cycle (twenty-eight days). After that, store it in a high cupboard. (It's okay to seal it in plastic if you're worried about ants.)

Obtain a New Job

There is no reason for you to face the job hunt without a bit of magic under your hat. This spell will not only open doors of opportunity and magnetize a job that is ideal for you, but will also breathe a whole lot more fun into the whole experience of finding a job.

Ingredients

A royal or navy blue candle in a jar or candle holder
An iron pyrite crystal, cleansed in bright sunlight for 2–3 minutes
Paper and pen
Your computer and resume-writing software
Computer paper and printer
A manila folder

It's ideal to do this ritual on a new moon or when the moon is waxing, but if you happen to be job hunting during the waning moon, that's fine too.

In the evening, light the candle. Close your eyes, breathe deeply, and center yourself while holding the pyrite in your right hand. When you feel calm and grounded, consider the ideal qualities that will be present in your new job. How much money would you be comfortable with? What area would you like the job to be in? How would you like to feel around your coworkers? What other qualities matter to you? Place the pyrite next to the paper and write this all down in the present tense, as if it's already true. Start with "I love my new job!" Then continue with the qualities, describing the job as if you already have it. Be as specific as possible about what really matters to you, but don't be so specific that you limit the universe's creativity. For example, if you write "I get to wear my cowboy hat at work," this will seriously narrow down the possibilities. Writing "I get to wear clothes that are both comfortable and attractive" will keep many more options open. Then again, if that cowboy hat is a deal breaker, write it down!

When you've perfectly fine-tuned the qualities you desire in your new job, conclude your list with "Thank you, universe! For all of this or something even better." Then sign and date.

Next, open up your resume (or a resume template if you don't have one already) and get it just right. In addition to including anything you would usually write, make sure that your stated objective is not about the job you want to obtain but rather the positivity and blessings you'd like to share with your new employer and customers. For example, let's say you'd like to find a position as a dance teacher. Instead of writing "Objective: to find a job teaching dance to children," you could write "Objective: to share the joy of dance and movement with children, and to ignite their self-esteem in the process." Or, if you'd like to find a position as a server at a restaurant, you could write "Objective: to offer a truly exceptional dining experience by listening to my customers and making genuine connections with them." Fine-tune your objective until it feels authentic to you and reminds you of how much you have to offer. Set the intention to remember this objective when writing cover letters and communicating with potential employers.

Print out your resume. Place it in the manila folder and set it on your altar or in another special place. Fold up the ideal job qualities, folding the paper toward you each time. Place it on top of the folder, and set the candle (in the holder) and the pyrite on top of the folded paper. Allow the candle to burn safely for at least one hour, then extinguish it.

The next day, make copies of your resume and begin your job hunt in earnest, keeping the pyrite with you (i.e., in your pocket or purse) at all times.

12

Enchanting Your Love Life

Let's get one thing straight right off the top: *A love spell performed for the purpose of controlling the affections of a specific person is a bad idea*. As you may recall, everything you send out returns to you multiplied. If you take away someone else's free will, guess what? At the least convenient moment, your freedom will be taken away in a reciprocal (and undoubtedly unpleasant) way.

However, provided you leave the identity of your beloved up to the universe, you can still use love magic to manifest anything your little heart desires! After all, it will work out much better for you anyway. All the love you're craving will still be there, just not (perhaps) with old what's-his-name.

All that being said, love magic is among the most exciting magic there is. After all, attraction itself is magical: it's a dynamic of all effective magic, and it's a precious, magical gift the Lord and Lady offer to us all.

Discover Your True Desires

When it comes to attraction and romance, what do you really want? Do you want to stay or go? Do you want to get serious or play the field? Do you want to date men, women, or both? Do you want to live with a partner or would you rather live alone? Are you even interested in romance right now? Do you know where your passion lies?

If the answers to any of these questions (or other ones about your love life) are currently eluding you, this spell will help you discover what you really want. And knowing what you want is of the utmost importance, because sexual power is magical power, and sexual clarity is magical clarity. What's more, the world shapes itself to reflect your clearly, confidently stated desires.

Caution: Don't do this spell on a work day, as it involves drinking wine in the morning!

Ingredients
1 stick or cone of rose incense and holder

A lighter or matches

2 wine glasses

Red wine

When the moon is between new and full, wake up before the sunrise and go outside. (You can find sunrise times in your area online.) Sit comfortably in a good sunrise-viewing spot, facing east. Breathe deeply, relax your body, and center your mind. As soon as the sun peeks over the horizon, light the incense to the sun. (If your area is fire-prone, be sure to take necessary precautions.) Also pour two glasses of wine, one for you and one for the sun. As the smoke rises toward the sky, raise your glass to the rising sun and say:

You make the world both warm and bright,
You set the morning sky alight.
To you this floral smoke I light,
As you rise and end the night.

Into my heart and soul now shine
My true desires now divine.
As we share this precious wine,
Reveal what I want as mine.

Drink your wine slowly and then pour the sun's libation onto the earth. Relax and feel supportive, clarifying light shining into your heart and illuminating your soul's most ideal unfolding. Your true desires will now make themselves known. Listen deeply.

Call In a New Romance

Ready for a new love to show up in your life? Call one in with this sweet and simple love spell.

Ingredients

2 pink ribbons, 1 yard each

1 red ribbon, 1 yard in length

A clear quartz crystal point, cleansed in bright sunlight

Relax and center yourself. Then consider all the ways you'd like to feel in your new romance: happy, beautiful, laughter-filled, excited, etc. Feel these feelings! Bring them totally into your being. Overflow with them, as if you are already in the throes of romantic bliss.

The pink ribbons symbolize you and your new love. The red ribbon symbolizes the passionate attraction you share. Continuing with the feelings associated with your new romance, tie the three ribbons together at one end with a simple knot. Then weave them into a braid. Secure the braid with another knot.

Wind the braid around the crystal and set it on your altar until your love appears in your life. (It's okay if the braid is not securely fastened to the crystal, or if it comes loose and you need to rewind it.) Then you can move the charm to a lingerie or nightstand drawer.

Repair a Relationship

The most effective way to work magic is to align with the best outcome for all concerned. From this perspective, it's not ideal to salvage every relationship. Some are best left broken, to leave space for an even better one to appear. Still, if a relationship can and should be repaired, this should do the trick. You can adapt this spell to repair a friendship or family relationship as well.

Ingredients

A stick or cone of high-quality sandalwood incense and holder

A picture of you and your partner (or former partner), cut in half
    so you appear separately

A Band-Aid

Ideally when the moon is between new and full, light the incense. Set the intention to heal your relationship in the most ideal possible way, whatever this may look like. In other words, if it's ultimately best for you to part ways, you will do that, but in the most healed and powerful possible way. On the other hand, if staying together is what's best, you'll do that.

Bathe the image of yourself in the smoke, feeling as you do that you are deeply healing your heart and attuning yourself to the frequency of harmonious love. Repeat this process with the image of your partner. Then repair the image by placing both halves back together and affixing the Band-Aid to the back. Finally, bathe the repaired image in the incense smoke, feeling that you are energetically reattuning the two of you to each other and deeply healing your relationship dynamic. Leave the repaired photo on your altar for one full moon cycle (twenty-eight days). Then store it with your other photos or dispose of it (whichever feels best to you).

Bless a Relationship

Any romance—new, old, or anywhere in between—can benefit from a relationship blessing ritual. This will, in essence, align your relationship with the purest expression of divine harmony and love. Like all ethical love spells, this one does not impose any specific design on the relationship. Rather, it encourages the relationship to unfold in whatever way is best for your soul's evolution as well as that of your partner.

You'll want to enlist your partner for this one. You can do it for just the two of you at home, or feature it as part of a wedding or handfasting ritual.

Do this ritual on a Friday when the moon is between new and full and ideally in Taurus or Libra.

Ingredients

2 naturally scented rose candles and holders

A stick or cone of rose incense and holder

Fresh petals from at least 12 red roses (in a basket or bowl)

A mister of rose water

Explain to your partner that you want to bless your relationship with the energy of divine harmony, sweetness, and love. If your partner agrees to participate, light the candles and incense. (It is not necessarily a red flag if your partner has no interest in magic, so don't be alarmed if he or she doesn't share your enthusiasm. I speak from experience.) Keep the candles and incense nearby as you sit or stand comfortably across from your partner. Relax and center yourselves as you gaze lovingly at each other. When you feel connected and grounded, scatter the rose petals in a circle around the two of you while moving in a clockwise direction. Then generously mist yourself, your partner, and the entire circle (as designated by the roses) with the rose water. Next, speak the following words. (I'm envisioning that you'll speak them on behalf of the both of you, but if your partner wants to join in, that's fine too.)

We now align this relationship with the highest and purest vibrations of divine harmony and love.

May this relationship bring waves of joy and bliss to our hearts.

May this relationship bring waves of grace and beauty to the world.

May this relationship be a force of sweetness, positivity, and healing on all levels and in all directions of time.

Thank you, thank you, thank you.

Blessed be. And so it is.

Give each other a hug and a kiss and hang out in this magical energy for a bit. Then extinguish the candles and incense, or allow them to safely burn all the way down. (Otherwise, you can relight them at intervals until they are safely burned all the way down.) Leave the rose petals for up to twenty-four hours, and then release them back to the earth or into a moving body of water. Save any remaining rose water for future magical use.

Attract Romantic Attention

Just as there is nothing unethical about wearing lipstick or perfume, there is nothing unethical about magically bolstering your natural radiance, magnetism, and allure. Your true self is blindingly beautiful anyway, so attractiveness magic is actually just you being you.

Perform this spell before attending any event or gathering during which you'd like to attract romantic attention in the most fun possible way. But please don't do it more than once per season, or it will lose its kick (so that's four times a year, max).

Also, you might want to refrain from doing this before someone else's wedding or birthday party. It's just, you know, good magical etiquette.

Ingredients
1 white or off-white soy candle and holder

1 stick Nag Champa incense and holder

1 cup of loose-leaf white tea, empowered in the light of a full moon for 5–10 minutes

As you draw a warm bath, light up your bathroom with nothing but the candle. Also light the incense. When the bathtub is full, scatter the tea across the top of the water. Stand over the tub, direct your palms toward the water, and visualize very bright golden-white light channeling down through the top of your head and up through the soles of your feet, meeting at your heart and then going down through your arms and hands and into the water. See the water as surrounded and filled with a brilliantly radiant miniature sun.

Get in the water and say:

I am like the moon: my cool radiance enraptures.
I am like the sun: around me all revolves.

Stay in the bath for ten to twenty minutes, feeling your irresistible radiance increasing and pulsating as you soak. The spell's effects will last for twelve to twenty-four hours.

Heal from a Breakup

The pain of a breakup can really smart. In addition to feelings of grief and loss, there can be other undesirable residuals, such as low self-esteem and a reluctance to open your heart to someone new. This spell will speed along the healing process and help you release the extra baggage sooner rather than later.

Please note that this spell can also be employed to help heal disordered eating or an unhealthy body image.

Ingredients
3 freshly cut spears from a thriving aloe plant
Scissors or gardening shears

During a waning moon and ideally not too long before bedtime, take a shower or bath. After drying off, leave your clothes off. Alternatively, wear nothing but a robe. Sit comfortably, take some deep breaths, and center yourself. When you feel ready, cut the first aloe spear into smaller pieces. Open up each piece so that the medicinal part of the aloe is visible. Then rub the wet, slimy side of each piece over your lower belly. As you do so, say:

I am healed and whole, lovingly nourished by the abundant earth.

Cut up the second aloe spear, and rub each piece over your solar plexus area (your upper belly area, above your bellybutton). This time, say:

I am healed and whole, one with the power that creates worlds.

Now cut up the third aloe spear, and rub each piece over your heart area. Say:

I am healed and whole: loved, loving, and lovable.

Relax for another moment, feeling the healing energy of the aloe sinking into your energetic being, establishing deep new patterns of wholeness within you. When you feel ready, wipe off the excess aloe with a warm washcloth and dress yourself in clean pajamas that you love. The next morning (or that same night if you have the energy), return the aloe pieces to the earth or release them in a moving body of water.

••• ◆ 13 ◆ •••

Beautifying and Harmonizing

In the religious paradigm that has predominated for centuries in the West, the conscious beautification of one's home or body (or really anything physical, except maybe a church or religious relic) is not considered to be a sacred activity. But this is a fallacy. After all, what is true beauty if not an intrinsic quality of the Divine? How would we recognize it or why would we seek it if it didn't resonate with the pure, unadulterated beauty that we sense is at the heart and soul of everything? Of course, when we think of the physical as separate from the spiritual, it results in beautification efforts that feel frivolous and shallow. On the other hand, when we beautify with reverence, we are aligning our outer experience of physicality with our inner experience of the God/Goddess/All That Is.

Fine-Tune the Vibrations in Your Home

When it comes to creating world peace, you might feel frustrated with the enormity of the task. But your home is your own personal corner of the planet, over which you reign with absolute power.

With this ritual, you *can* establish world peace, starting with your realm.

Before performing this ritual, be sure to clear clutter and physically clean your home. Optionally, give your home a good smudge with white or desert sage before you begin (see chapter 9).

Ingredients

A mister of rose water

A very small labradorite crystal, cleansed in running water and sunlight

A melodious chime or bell

Place all ingredients in a central or prominent place in your home. Standing near them, center yourself and take some deep breaths. Then set the clear intention to establish peace by saying:

I now attune the vibrations of my home to the purest frequencies of harmony and love.

Open the mister of rose water and drop the crystal in it. Close it back up and set it aside.

Move around the perimeter of each room and area in your home in a generally clockwise direction. As you do so, sound the chime or bell. With each sound current, see/imagine/sense vibrations of clarity, harmony, and love moving outward and shifting the molecules of your home in the most positive possible way.

Then move through each room and area again in the same way, this time with the rose water, misting each space generously as you go. With each spray, see/imagine/sense the vibrations of your home becoming even more finely calibrated to the energies of pure positivity and love.

Finally, stand again in the central and/or prominent location. With your spine straight and feet planted firmly on the earth, hold your hands in prayer pose. Close your eyes and take some deep breaths. Then visualize a sphere of rainbow light completely filling and surrounding your home. See it begin to move slowly in a clockwise direction. Imagine this light further balancing and calibrating your home's energy while holding all these harmonious vibrations in place. Say:

Thank you, thank you, thank you.
Blessed be. And so it is.

Get More Beautiful with Age

Your beliefs and expectations shape your experiences. As such, the only way for your beauty to diminish with age is if you buy into the myth that it must. It's a myth that has duped a lot of people over the years, but it needn't dupe you—particularly if you perform this ritual and expect precisely the reverse to be true.

Ingredients
A soy candle and holder
A black actinolite crystal, cleansed in running water and sunlight
Crab apple flower essence (available at most health food stores)
A water bottle that you love, filled with drinking water

At the new moon, shower or bathe, then dress in clean clothes, eveningwear, or lingerie that you love.

Light the candle. Relax and take some deep breaths.

Hold the crystal above the flame so that it's gently warmed and illuminated. As you do so, say:

With each passing year, my radiance brightens
and my beauty deepens.

Set the crystal down near the candle.

Add three drops of the crab apple flower essence to the water, and say:

I officially recognize and believe in my radiant beauty,
which continually increases in dimension and intensity.

Take a good, large gulp of the water. Feel it filling your body with radiant light and illuminating your mind with the firm belief and expectation that your beauty will continually increase.

Inwardly commit to taking meticulous care of yourself in the most loving way possible, by drinking lots of water, eating healthful and nourishing foods, getting plenty of sleep, wearing things you feel great in, etc.

Say:

Thank you, thank you, thank you.
Blessed be. And so it is.

Drink the rest of the water before the day is over. For at least two moon cycles (that's fifty-six days), keep the crystal under your pillow while you sleep and place it on a sunny windowsill during the day. Also for at least two moon cycles, drink one full bottle of water each day, to which you've added three drops of crab apple essence.

Activate Your Radiance

True story: as a child of the God and Goddess, you are naturally, strikingly gorgeous. This ritual will activate the blinding radiance that lies within you, so your enchanting beauty will shine like a lighthouse beacon for all to see and enjoy.

Ingredients

Champagne or sparkling water

A wine glass, champagne flute, or chalice

Sunflower flower essence (available from Fesflowers.com)

Moonstone gem elixir (available from AlaskanEssences.com)

When the full moon is bright in the sky, bathe and then dress in clean clothes, evening wear, or lingerie in which you feel both comfortable and beautiful (or go skyclad, aka completely nude).

Relax and take some deep breaths.

Pour yourself a glass of champagne or sparkling water. Add one drop of sunflower essence and two drops of moonstone elixir. While holding the potion, close your eyes and feel that you are the sun, radiating your beauty for all to see and enjoy. Next, feel that you are the moon, luxuriously soaking in the golden-white light of the sun. Feel these two energies mingling in your glass as you say:

Father Sun and Mother Moon,
I lovingly request this boon:
Arouse within my soul's true light,
So my beauty shines forth day and night.

Mindfully drink the potion. With each sip, feel your radiant beauty awakening more and more. Then, with immense gratitude and excitement for the success of your ritual, say:

Thank you, thank you, thank you.
Blessed be. And so it is.

Balance Your Body Weight

Let's face it: our culture is downright dysfunctional when it comes to food, weight, and body image. So it's no wonder so many of us seem to be challenged by this particular aspect of our physicality. This spell will help you reach a healthy weight without starving yourself, subscribing to any harmful fads, or obsessing over the number on the scale.

Ingredients

A blue or turquoise soy candle and holder

Essential oil of neroli (in a carrier oil if your skin is sensitive)

A rose quartz crystal, cleansed with bright sunlight for at least 5
    minutes

A red jasper crystal, cleansed the same way

On the day or evening of a new moon, light the candle. Take a few deep breaths and come into the moment.

Anoint your forehead and wrists with the essential oil. (If your skin is sensitive, be sure to dilute it as necessary with a carrier oil, such as sunflower or sweet almond.)

Hold the rose quartz to your heart with your left hand, and hold the jasper against your lower belly with your right hand. Take some deep breaths. When you feel relaxed and centered, say:

> *I love myself.*
> *I approve of myself.*
> *I am safe.*
> *I am loved and lovable.*
> *I am valuable and valid.*
> *At all times and under all circumstances, I am my own loyal ally.*

Set the crystals near the candle. Repeat the anointing and affirming process, as described here, once daily for the next twenty-eight days (one full moon cycle).

Harmonize Your Thoughts

If your thoughts feel discordant or scattered, harmonize them with this simple soul-nourishing spell.

Ingredient

A lepidolite pendant

On the day of a new moon, visit a moving body of water. Bathe the lepidolite pendant in the rushing water or waves. As you do so, feel that you are bathing your thoughts: releasing what doesn't serve you and purifying your mental landscape. Remove the pendant from the water and hold it in your right hand. Allow it to air-dry as you relax and gaze at the water for another mindful moment.

Then wear the pendant. Continue wearing it as frequently as possible for at least one full moon cycle (i.e., until the next new moon).

··· ◆ 14 ◆ ···

Blessing and Protecting

To bless something is to imbue it with divine energy and to attune its vibration to the frequency of infinite love. This has a naturally protective side effect, as like attracts like. It also helps that which has been blessed to experience what we commonly refer to as *luck*: a generous flow of fortuitous and favorable conditions.

Bless Your Home

If your home is new (or just new to you), you haven't blessed it before, or it's time for a vibrational shift or an energetic upgrade, it's a good idea to perform this ritual. It's simple, but it's so, so effective.

It's best to do this when your house is clean and tidy.

Ingredients
Fresh petals from at least 12 red roses (in a basket or bowl)
9 sticks of sandalwood incense
A lighter or matches
A dish or plate

On a new moon, assemble the ingredients near your altar, in a central location or in another location that feels appropriate (such as the fireplace or the entry). Sit or stand with your spine straight, close your eyes, and take some deep breaths to ground and center yourself.

When you feel ready, invoke the Divine in a way that feels powerful for you, and ask for a strong infusion of love and light to fill your home. Also speak words from your heart about what type of energies and conditions you're calling into your space. Then feel gratitude, knowing that your words have been heard and are being acted upon. While still feeling gratitude, say *thank you* nine times. (You can keep count by saying it three times three.)

While holding the receptacle containing the rose petals, move in a generally clockwise direction around the inside perimeter of your home, scattering petals across every doorway and windowpane that borders the outside. Repeat on any additional floors.

Next, safely light all nine sticks of incense and hold them together over the dish or plate in such a way that you'll be sure to catch any burning embers. Move in a generally clockwise direction throughout each room and area of your space, wafting the smoke around generously as you go.

Safely extinguish the incense. (You can do this by sealing it in a jar or immersing the smoldering ends in water.)

Stand again in the location where you assembled the ingredients, and feel gratitude once again for all the divine energy you've just successfully called in. Once more, say *thank you* nine times.

Leave the rose petals for at least twenty-four hours, and then return them to the earth by releasing them in a natural body of water or placing them near the base of a tree. Feel free to burn any of the partially burned incense for any future magical or aromatherapeutic purposes.

Protect Your Home

This single-ingredient spell is an extremely powerful way to protect your home from all forms of harm, misfortune, and ill will. But I still recommend taking concrete, commonsense steps to keep everyone in your home safe, such as locking the door and blowing out candles before you leave the house. After all, the safest homes are the ones protected in both realms: spiritual and physical.

Ingredient

About 4 ounces hydrangea root powder in a white ceramic bowl

On a Sunday when the moon is anywhere between second quarter and full, empower the hydrangea root powder by holding the bowl in the bright light of the sun. As you do so, imagine it absorbing bright, protective, negativity-incinerating vibrations. After two to five minutes, walk around the outside perimeter of your house in a clockwise direction, sprinkling the powder on the ground as you go. If you live in an apartment or this is otherwise not possible, you can simply sprinkle it in front of any doors that lead to the outside, and also in front of any windows to which you have outdoor access.

Cocoon Yourself in Positivity

One of the questions I get most often is some variation of "How do you keep your energy positive around challenging people?" Indeed, who among us hasn't, at one time or another, asked ourselves this very thing?

The late, great spiritual author Wayne Dyer said it well: "How people treat you is their karma; how you react is yours." This ritual will fortify your healthy boundaries while cocooning you in soft, sweet energy. When you are thus shielded, other people's karma need not encroach on yours.

Admittedly, this ritual takes work, but it's worth it. Plus, the time you put into it doubles as an excellent morning meditation.

Ingredients

A mala (prayer beads) made with 108 rose quartz beads (You can purchase one or make your own.)

Alternatively, you can use a simple necklace made with 108 rose quartz beads, as long as there's some type of marker (such as a tassel or clasp) that will allow you to keep count.

First, spiritually cleanse the mala or necklace in bright sunlight, white sage smoke, and/or running water. Ideally, also empower it in the light of the full moon (but don't delay your spell for the full moon's sake—you can always empower it later).

Every morning before you leave the house, sit facing east, with your spine straight in a comfortable way. Take some deep breaths and center your mind.

Using the beads to keep count, chant *Om shrim* 108 times. Before you begin, chant simply *Om*. After your 108th repetition, chant *Om* once more.

Om aligns you with the Divine/Infinity/All That Is. *Shrim* aligns you with good fortune, luxury, order, balance, and harmonious love. As you chant, consciously send the vibration of each sound throughout your physical body and aura. If your mind wanders, simply bring it back.

After your final Om, rest in the positive energy you've summoned. Sense/imagine/feel it as a sweet pink light filling and surrounding you.

Wear the necklace throughout the day to protect and preserve the positive energy you've summoned.

Bless a Baby

A baby is an emissary newly crossed over into our realm from the realm of light. How magical! To bless a baby's newly incarnated form and to clear the way for the most magical life momentum possible, perform the following ritual.

Ingredients
A fresh lavender blossom
An attractive glass containing a small amount of water
Fresh petals from 3 red roses

While standing outdoors in bright sunlight, place the lavender blossom in the water. Allow the water to absorb the sunlight for five to ten minutes, making sure that no shadows pass over it.

Ideally while the baby is sleeping (or at least not crying), scatter the rose petals around the child in a clockwise direction. Then anoint the baby's forehead with a little of the water from the glass.

While keeping a close eye to make sure the rose petals don't pose a choking hazard, say:

> God/Goddess/All That Is, bless this child. May his/her life be filled
> with magic, joy, and all good things. May he/she know himself/her-
> self as the divine and powerful being he/she is in truth. Thank you.

To further bless the baby, cleanse and consecrate the child's room or sleeping area by using the lavender blossom to fling tiny bits of the water around the perimeter of the room.

Gather up the rose petals, and when you have a moment, return them to the earth by placing them at the base of a tree. Also place the lavender blossom at the base of a tree, and pour out any remaining water there as well.

Protect Your Child or Animal Friend

If you've taken every safety precaution in the world and you're still worried about the wellbeing of your child or pet, this ritual will help by providing your beloved one with an extra dose of magical protection. It employs angelic energy to create a powerful shield of light and love, which helps protect from dangers in both the seen and the unseen world.

Ingredients
A photo of your child or pet
1 white or off-white candle and holder
Essential oil of angelica
2 tablespoons angelica root
1 tablespoon sea salt
A small glass or ceramic bowl
A spoon or other stirring device

Place the photo on your altar, with the candle nearby. Light the candle. Say:

> *Archangel Michael, I call on you.*
> *Archangel Raphael, I call on you.*

Anoint the photo with a tiny bit of the essential oil. Say:

> *Thank you for watching over [name of child or pet].*
> *Thank you for keeping him/her safe from all dangers:*
> *inner and outer, seen and unseen.*

Mix the angelica root and sea salt together in the bowl with the spoon or other stirring device. Sprinkle the mixture in a circle around the photo. Visualize your child or pet completely surrounded in a sphere of protective white light. Say:

Thank you, thank you, thank you.
Blessed be. And so it is.

Extinguish the candle. Leave the sprinkled mixture for at least twenty-four hours and then dispose of it. Repeat once per moon cycle as desired, or just refresh the magic by calling on Archangel Michael and Archangel Raphael regularly to protect and watch over your little one.

Bless a Business

This blessing spell draws its considerable power from the African-American folk saint John the Conqueror, an ally who brings many blessings, including abundance, wealth, luck, victory, and protection. While the details of his origin story are not entirely clear, in the words of author Judika Illes in her book *Encyclopedia of Mystics, Saints & Sages*, John the Conqueror "may have been born in Africa or he may have been born on an American plantation, the son of an African prince. Some consider him an avatar of the African trickster spirit Eshu-Elegbara."

He also shares his name (and energy) with a root, so don't be confused by the ingredients list.

Ingredients

1 John the Conqueror root (Find this at bulk herb stores in your
    neighborhood or online.)
1 John the Conqueror candle and holder (There are many options
    online and at magical supply stores, so just find one you like, or
    make your own.)
A small garden shovel
2 bottles champagne or sparkling cider

Before the ritual, empower the root in bright sunlight for two to five minutes.

If your business consists of more people than just you, host a casual gathering. Invite anyone you feel should be there to help bless the business, such as founders, partners, and/or assistants. Before they arrive, assemble the ingredients and light the candle. Say:

> John the Conqueror, I call on you. Please share with this business your wisdom, power, and cunning, and bless it with amazing and ongoing good fortune. Thank you.

Use the shovel to bury the root outside near the front door to the business (or your home, if it's a home-based business). If there's no soil near the door, bury it in a potted plant. If it's not possible to place a plant outside the front door, you can also bury it in an indoor potted plant near the door.

Also open one of the bottles of champagne or cider, and pour it onto the earth near the front door of the business as a libation and gratitude offering to John the Conqueror. If this is not appropriate or possible, find the closest tree and pour it out around the roots.

Once your colleagues arrive (or just by yourself, if no one else is invited), open the second bottle of champagne or cider. Pour a glass for everyone present and make a toast summarizing some of the blessings John the Conqueror bestows. Say:

> May this business and everyone in it be blessed with joy, victory, success, luck, power, prosperity, and every wonderful thing!
> To John the Conqueror!

Then drink. (If anyone asks you who John the Conqueror is, feel free to tell them. Or you can just act mysterious about it. Your call.)

15

Binding and Banishing

When it comes to working ethical magic (aka magic that won't contaminate your karma), binding and banishing can be a bit tricky. But tricky doesn't mean impossible! In fact, as long as you follow these three guidelines, you're good:

1. Stay neutral—i.e., don't work magic from a place of anger or a desire for retribution. It's okay to feel these feelings in your everyday life, but once you step into your ritual space, be like a bamboo flute: let magical energy flow through you without letting your personal feelings encroach.

2. Focus on the other person only as they relate to you. In other words, if someone is encroaching on *your* free will, you have every right to work magic to stop them from continuing to do so. So set the intention to interfere in their energy *only in order to protect and preserve your own natural right to thrive.* Then stop there.

3. Be sure to bind or banish only as a last resort, and to bind or banish only *bullies*: those who consciously and purposefully use their power to hurt, subdue, intimidate, or otherwise unfairly encroach upon our free will.

All that being said, the term *binding* (as we're using it here) means to effectively nullify someone's power in one or more life areas. Imagine putting someone in a strait jacket, or putting them in handcuffs, in order to keep them from causing you harm.

Banishing means to get someone out of your life, space, or energy field, and to keep them from returning. It's sort of like a restraining order, insect repellent, and an electric fence all tied into one.

Bind Someone's Power to Cause You Physical Harm

This spell is for binding the classic bully: the individual who threatens you with physical injury.

Ingredients

A black candle and holder

Paper and pen

A Sharpie or similar black marker

A small bit of fresh leek

A mortar and pestle

Strong hemp twine

Scissors

Sea salt

A small jar with a tight lid

Light the candle. On the paper, write the bully's name with the pen. It's best if you can find out their full name, but if you can't, just write whatever you know. Then using the black marker, cross out the name decisively with an X. As you do so, say:

You have no power to hurt me, physically or otherwise.

Put the leek in the mortar and grind with the pestle until you have a pungent green paste. Smear the paste over the name with the X over it. As you do so, say:

You are now completely harmless and unthreatening to me. Your power to hurt me is not just weak, it is completely void. It is as nothing. It is as if it has never existed.

Roll up the paper into a little scroll, making sure to roll it away from you. Then tie it tightly with a piece of hemp twine, making a double knot. As you do so, say:

[Name of bully], I bind you.

Repeat with eight more pieces of twine, to make nine total ties.

Pour some sea salt in the jar, put the bound scroll in the jar as well, and then fill the jar the rest of the way with sea salt, so that the scroll is completely immersed in the salt. Say:

Your power to hurt me is now bound and neutralized.

Close the jar with the lid and extinguish the candle.

Dispose of the remaining leek as you normally would. Save the remaining candle for future magical use.

Store the jar in your freezer until you no longer feel the need to keep this person bound. Then flush the salt down the toilet, throw the scroll in the trash, and recycle the jar.

Bind Someone's Power to Cause You Spiritual Harm

Here are some words to live by: Do everything you can to avoid getting into a metaphysical tangle with another magic worker. Under no circumstances should you be looking to pick any supernatural fights. While magic can certainly come in handy when it comes to psychic self-defense, using it to prop up your ego or to prove your power will never end well for you. At worst it will summon a karmic takedown. At best it will leave you feeling hollow, bitter, and sad. (You'll notice this book teaches how to protect yourself from hexes and curses but not how to perform them.)

That being said, some people do, unfortunately, cast predatory (or otherwise unethical) spells on other people. In addition to hexes and curses, this includes love spells or spells to induce lust that purposely disregard and override your free will. Other spiritual bullying can come in the form of unwelcome psychic vampiring or cording (i.e., draining your personal energy without your consent).

But don't panic! First of all, if you faithfully do your daily clearing and shielding exercises (see chapter 6), you're already ahead of the game. Second, you can employ the information in the next chapter to break hexes and love spells, and transmute negative energy into positive energy. And finally, if you feel the need to bind a particular person from causing you any further spiritual harm, this ritual has got you covered.

Ingredients
A black candle and holder

A picture of the person to bind (printed out from the internet is fine)

Strong black string or twine
A small jar with a tight lid
Enough garlic powder to fill the jar
1 tablespoon dried huckleberry leaf

Light the candle. Fold or roll up the photo, rolling away from you. Bundle it up by tying it tightly with the black twine as you say:

[Name of person], your magic has no power over me.

Tie it with another piece of the twine as you say:

[Name of person], I bind you from causing me harm, in any realm: physical, spiritual, mental, or emotional.

Tie it with one more piece of twine and say:

[Name of person], your power to harm me has never existed in truth, and it now goes back to its native nothingness, and is null and void forever and ever, in all directions of time.

Pour some of the garlic powder in the jar. Place the bound bundle on top of it. Cover it with the huckleberry leaf. Then fill the jar the rest of the way with garlic powder. Close the lid tightly and say:

[Name of person], I bind you.
[Name of person], I bind you.
[Name of person], I bind you.

Pay a visit to a public trash can or dump at least ten miles from your home, and throw away the jar. As you depart from the disposal site, don't look back. As soon as possible, go home, throw the clothes you're wearing in the wash machine, take a shower or bath, and dress in something clean and fresh.

Bind Someone's Power to Cause You Legal Harm

There are, unfortunately, individuals who are not above employing the law or the legal system in an unfair, petty, or malicious way. But never fear, my dear, because you have something they didn't bargain on. You have magic on your side.

Ingredients

A white candle and holder

Something on paper to symbolize the person or group to bind, such as their full name (and full birth date if you know it), business card, photo, or something else powerfully attuned to their energy

Hemp twine

A glass bottle with a cork

9 nails

9 whole cloves

White vinegar

Light the candle. Place the paper representation of the person or group nearby. Say:

> *Forseti, lord of fairness and justice, hail, hail, hail.*
>
> *Over he/she/they who seek(s) to cause me harm,*
> *prevail, prevail, prevail.*

Using your fist like a gavel, pound the paper representation firmly nine times, feeling that you are stamping out any appearance of power this person or group has over you, and that your fairness is easily overcoming their falseness.

Now roll or fold the paper up into a small package, being sure to roll or fold away from you. Then tie it tightly with the hemp twine three times (using three separate pieces of twine). With each tie, say:

> All illusions of false power are now bound from causing me harm or the appearance of harm. My power is divine power: endless, boundless, and inexhaustible.

Put the bundle in the bottle. Add the nails and cloves to the bottle, and fill it the rest of the way with the vinegar. Then cork it. Say:

> [Name of person or group] has zero power to harm me, now or ever.
> Forseti, lord of fairness and justice,
> Thank you, thank you, thank you.
> Blessed be. And so it is.

Keep the bottle in a safe place until all legal disputes or potential legal disputes have come to an agreeable end.

Banish a Pesky Ex

As humans, we all crave appreciation and attention. But in certain cases involving certain people, we want the exact opposite: we just want to be left alone. This banishing spell is designed to get a pesky ex-partner to stop bothering you and get out of your life for good.

Ingredients
A small piece of paper and a pen
A cauldron or pot in which you can safely burn the paper
A lighter or matches
A half-pint (8-ounce) Mason jar filled almost to the top with water

Write the full name (or as much of it as you know) of the ex-partner on the paper. Crumple it lightly, place it in the cauldron, and light it on fire. As it burns, say:

Your feelings are like fire and they now burn themselves out.

Your presence in my life is now purified and demolished in the cleansing flame.

If necessary, relight until the paper is mostly or completely reduced to ashes.

Pour the water over the ashes and say:

Your feelings were like fire and they are now extinguished.

Your presence in my life now flows away from me forever.

Swirl up the mixture and pour it back into the jar. Close the lid tightly and put it in your freezer. Close the freezer door and say:

The fire is now ice, and the fire is gone, and it is as if it has never been. You are now banished from my life. I shall not hear from you, see you, or think of you. You are gone from me—invisible, frozen out—and I have already forgotten who you are.

To keep the magic strong, do not contact this person in any way or even speak of them. Truly behave as if they do not exist to you. Once you feel the threat of them coming back has passed, you can thaw out the jar, flush the ashy water down the toilet, and recycle.

Banish an Unwanted Houseguest

You might be surprised to learn that getting rid of an unwanted houseguest (or anyone who has overstayed their welcome) is a common and classic magical aim, because there are times when asking someone to leave—or even *telling* them to leave—just doesn't work quite like it should.

Perform this ritual when your houseguest is out of the house.

Ingredients
4 heads of fresh garlic
A clean bucket
White vinegar
Tap water
Clean rags
Essential oil of angelica

Moving in a counterclockwise direction, place one head of garlic in each of the four corners of your home. (Obviously, not everyone's home will be a perfect rectangle or square, so just do your best to approximate.) With the first head of garlic, say:

[Name of houseguest], you are no longer comfortable in this home.

With the second head, say:

[Name of houseguest], you can't bear to stay within these walls another minute.

With the third head, say:

[Name of houseguest], I wish you well on your journey.

With the fourth head, say:

And, [name of houseguest], now you must go.

In the bucket, mix equal parts white vinegar and tap water. Again moving in a counterclockwise direction throughout your home, use this solution to thoroughly clean each and every window, inside and out. As you do so, feel that you are scrubbing your houseguest's presence out of your home. Replace the solution as necessary. Repeat on any additional floors.

Using the same 1:1 ratio of vinegar and tap water, also wash your front door, inside and out, and any other doors that border the outside.

Finally, put a single drop of angelica oil on each side of your houseguest's pillow. If any of their shoes happen to be in the house, put a single drop in each shoe as well.

If you're worried about fielding questions, answering with another question is always a good plan. For example, if your houseguest asks why there's garlic in the corner, you can say, "Haven't you ever heard of putting garlic in the corners for luck?" And if they ask why their pillow smells like herbs, you can just say, "Does it? How odd! What kind of herb does it smell like?"

Your houseguest should be gone within a week. When you're sure they're not coming back, dispose of the garlic in a compost pile or at the base of a tree.

Banish General Negativity and Bad Vibes

Maybe you don't know exactly what it is you need to banish, but you know it falls in the category of negativity. Luckily, you don't need to know its origin. Whether it's a space that still holds energy from previous tenants, negative thoughts that are consistently being sent your way, a malicious magic worker's bad mojo, or any other bad vibey-ness, this ritual will banish negativity from a home, business, or other physical space.

Ingredients
A white or off-white soy candle and holder (optional)
Plenty of sea salt in a bowl

A grapefruit

A cutting board and knife

4 clear quartz crystal points, cleansed in bright sunlight for at least
5–10 minutes

A selenite crystal or wand, cleansed in bright sunlight for at least
5–10 minutes

If you have pets in the space, arrange for them to be somewhere else during the ritual.

Light the candle, if you've got one. Open all the windows and doors. Now move around each room and area in a counterclockwise direction, decisively throwing generous handfuls of sea salt at the walls and in the corners as you go. As you do this, feel and sense that you are powerfully cleansing the home of negativity by both neutralizing and repelling it. Repeat on any additional floors.

Cut the grapefruit into four quarters. Go outside, and moving in a clockwise direction this time, visit all four corners of your home or property (whichever feels right). If you're in an apartment, or the four corners are difficult to reach or discern, just approximate them as best you can. At each corner, squeeze one grapefruit quarter so the juice drips onto the ground, then leave the remaining quarter on the ground with the juice. As you do this, feel and sense that you are decisively setting a boundary of positivity, through which only clean, fresh, loving energy may enter, and in which only such energy may remain.

Go back inside and wash your hands if they're sticky. Next, move around the inside of the space, visiting all four corners (or approximating them as best you can). At each corner, place one of the quartz crystal points. As you do so, feel that you are reinforcing the boundary of positivity and protection. (If you have additional floors, you only need to do this on one floor.)

Finally, with the selenite crystal in hand, move around each room and area in a generally clockwise direction. Intuitively wave the crystal around like a magic wand, recalibrating and reharmonizing the energy as you go.

If possible, leave the salt for twelve to twenty-four hours before sweeping or vacuuming it up. Also leave the grapefruit quarters for a similar amount of time before composting them, burying them, or placing them in your yard waste bin. The crystals can also stay in place for twelve to twenty-four hours, after which they can be cleansed (in sunlight, sage smoke, and/or running water) and stored for future magical work.

16

Breaking Hexes and Transmuting Negative Energy

I really don't want the title of this chapter to scare you.

First of all, chances are, no one will ever cast a malicious spell on you. Second of all, even if they do, you can transmute it to high heaven: you can take the negative momentum and redirect it into something that ultimately turns out to be wonderful for you. Seriously. It's a magical law: the law of transmutation.

The same is true for negative energy of all varieties. It need never be something to resist or run from. Rather, you can think of it as very dry kindling for your very bright fire, burning up completely while powerfully fueling your flame of positivity and love.

Break a Hex or a Curse

If you believe you have been the target of a hex or a curse, or even if you just suspect it, this spell will break it.

Ingredients

2 cups sea salt

A bundle of dried white sage, with a dish to catch burning embers

An image of the Hindu goddess Kali (a statue, a framed picture, or
even a postcard picture or a picture printed out from the internet)

A black candle and holder

Copal incense and holder

A mala, preferably with black beads (prayer beads with 108 beads
and a tassel, available online and at many import and metaphysical supply stores)

The day after a full moon, draw a warm or hot bath. Dissolve the
sea salt in the water and soak for at least forty minutes, being sure
to stay hydrated with plenty of drinking water.

Dry off and dress in clean white clothes, or don't wear anything
at all. Light the sage bundle so it's smoking like incense, and safely
smudge yourself by letting the smoke thoroughly waft around
your body and energy field. (Be sure to hold the dish under the
bundle to catch any burning embers.) Then smudge your entire
home, moving in a counterclockwise direction through each room
and area.

Create a small altar to Kali by lighting the candle and incense
near her image. Sit comfortably in front of the altar, possibly on
a cushion, with your spine relatively straight. Take some deep
breaths and relax. When you feel ready, chant to Kali, using the
prayer beads to keep count.

Start by chanting one time:

Om.

Then once per bead, for a total of 108 times, chant:

Om Klim Kalika-Yei Namaha.

Then chant one final time:

Om.

Drape the mala around your neck. Allow the incense to burn all the way down, then extinguish the candle. You should already be well on your way to a completely neutralized curse, but just for good measure, relight the candle and repeat the chant again each day until the new moon. Also wear the mala as much as you can until you're sure the hex is completely out of your energy field.

Redirect a Hex or a Curse

You can't go wrong with this spell if you set the intention simply to send any and all negative vibes right back to the sender(s). It doesn't get any fairer than that.

Ingredients

4 small square or rectangular mirrors (Inexpensive mirrors from a craft store will do.)

A spray bottle or mister filled with 1 part water and 1 part white vinegar

A clean white cloth

4 picture or diploma stands that will hold the mirrors (Try dollar or discount stores.)

44 fresh rosemary sprigs

Wash each mirror with the vinegar solution and cloth. Position the picture stands around you at the four cardinal directions (using a compass if necessary), facing out. Then place the mirrors on the stands so that they're all facing away from you.

Next, while moving in a counterclockwise direction, connect the mirrors by generously scattering the sprigs of rosemary in a circle. (The diameter could be approximately four to five feet.)

Sit in the center of the circle and relax. Feel all negativity drain out of your field and into the mirrors, and sense that any additional negativity being sent your way is being caught in the mirrors before entering the circle. Then visualize/imagine/sense that all energy trapped or held by the mirrors is instantly and powerfully beamed back to the sender, never to return again.

Nine times, say:

I am clear.

Nine times, say:

I am safe.

Nine times, say:

All is well.

Then finish with:

Thank you, thank you, thank you.
Blessed be. And so it is.

Stand up and turn in a counterclockwise circle nine times. Then crouch down and touch the floor with both palms.

Return the rosemary to the earth by releasing it in a moving body of water or placing it at the base of a tree. Wash the mirrors one more time with the cloth and vinegar solution, and donate them to a thrift store. Save the cleaning solution for future glass cleaning, or pour it down the drain.

Break a Love Spell (Or Just Get Over a Crush)

Do you suspect you may be the victim of a love spell? The nerve! But don't worry, you've got this. This spell won't be comfortable, but it *will* be worth it.

This spell can also be used to get over anyone you're really not into being into anymore.

Ingredients

1 cup dried hops

1 cup sea salt

2 cups fresh sage leaves

1 tablespoon pistachio extract

When the moon is waning, draw a cold bath. Add all the ingredients to the water. Stir the water in a counterclockwise direction until the salt is dissolved. Soak for at least forty minutes.

Before draining the water, remove the solid ingredients from the tub, and (later, once you're dressed) compost or place them at the base of a tree.

After that, the spell is over, but I do recommend putting on clean but totally unsexy pajamas and watching at least four episodes of *Seinfeld* by yourself, or possibly *Adventure Time*. *Sherlock* would also work. (Or something else! The idea here is to relax while occupying your mind with something funny and/or cerebral and not overly romantic.)

Bust Out of a Rut

One of the many perks of the magical path is that you need never feel like a victim again. This includes being a victim of stuck, stale, or stagnant energy, also known as *being in a rut*.

In addition to releasing feelings of stuckness or depression, this spell can help you move forward with specific projects or goals that seem to have stalled or come to a standstill.

Ingredients

A statue or figure of (the Hindu elephant-headed deity) Ganesh, any size

A fresh bright red flower of any variety in water (extra points if it's hibiscus or rose)

A red candle and holder

Patchouli or sandalwood incense and holder

First, clear clutter from your house and clean it thoroughly, making sure to drink a whole lot of clean, fresh water as you do so. Then create an altar to Ganesh with all the ingredients. Light the candle and incense. To align with Ganesha's proactive, organizing, rut-busting, obstacle-removing energy, say nine times:

Om Gam Ganapataye Namaha.

Allow the incense to burn all the way down as you do other things, and then extinguish the candle. Repeat this spell every day until your rut is busted and you're in the flow of a highly positive, joyful life momentum. Be sure to replace the candle and flower as necessary.

Transform a Problem into a Blessing

Have you ever stopped to think about how many possibilities for blessings there are in seeming problems? For example, if your future soul mate happens to be getting his car fixed, then getting a flat tire could be the best thing that ever happened to you. Even the most dire and heartbreaking problems have inspired world-changing inventions, perspectives, and works of art.

This spell will help activate the blessing potential within a problem. Try it when you feel stuck about how to move forward in any life area, or any time you can't seem to find your way out of a stubborn or perplexing challenge.

Ingredients

An ice cube tray

2 teaspoons baking soda, for each problem you want to transform

Water

A butter knife

A quart-size Mason jar (or larger)

Red and blue food coloring

White vinegar

Place two teaspoons baking soda in a single cube in the ice cube tray. (Make a cube for each problem you want to transform.) Fill each cube the rest of the way with water and stir with the butter knife until somewhat dissolved. Freeze overnight.

Wake up before sunrise. As the sun is rising, place the ice cube(s) in the jar. Put one drop of red and one drop of blue food coloring in the jar as well. (I have also used one drop teal and one drop magenta when I had the fancy-colored food dye.) Making sure you're someplace where you won't mind making a mess, pour the vinegar in the jar over all of it until covered. As the cubes froth and dissolve, say:

> *What was solid now bubbles and flows.*
> *Blessings arise, problem goes.*

Pour more vinegar as needed if you'd like to speed the dissolving process, enjoying the appearance of the purple froth. Continue until all the ice is transformed. Then rinse and clean everything as needed.

17

Healing Yourself and Others

Chances are good that you have a particular affinity for the healing mysteries. In ancient times, it's quite possible you would have been known as a shaman, wise one, or healing priestess. It's even possible you have lived one or more such lives.

Can you imagine it? Perhaps you gathered and dried herbs, gazed into the steam of your bubbling cauldron, spoke prophecies and omens, and created charms to help heal various ailments of mind, body, and spirit.

While the times and tools may have changed, your wisdom and power remain. In truth, modern magic workers are not that different from our ancient counterparts. As we reclaim our pride in our identity, we also reclaim our ability to heal.

Our natural state is one of wholeness and health, a result of a harmonious alignment with the cosmic and earthly energies. Healing is simply a process of realigning with this intrinsic wellness.

Bolster Your Immunity

If you seem to catch more than your fair share of cold and flu bugs, or perhaps find yourself with a sore throat or sinus infection that's been hanging on for much too long, it may be time for a magical immunity boost.

Perform this ritual in the evening, when you don't have anything else planned.

Ingredients
1 head of fresh garlic
5 sprigs fresh rosemary
A mortar and pestle
A white or off-white soy candle and holder
½ cup sea salt
Plenty of drinking water

Break the garlic into cloves and peel each one down to its shiny, white flesh. Muddle the rosemary by lightly crushing it with the mortar and pestle. Light the candle and draw a warm bath. Add the garlic, rosemary, and sea salt, and stir the water in a clockwise direction with your right hand. As you stir, envision the water glowing and pulsating with vibrant golden-white light.

Soak for twenty to forty minutes as you feel your body absorbing the strong, healthy energy of the herbs. Drink plenty of water as you soak. Afterward, dress in clean pajamas and get a good night's sleep. (At your convenience, compost the herbs or place them at the base of a tree.)

For at least thirty days afterward, have absolutely *no dairy products of any kind,* as dairy generates excessive mucus and inflammation in the body. Also consider cutting out all refined sugar and flour, or at least go very light on it. And naturally, be sure to drink lots of pure water, eat plenty of healthy food, and get lots of quality sleep.

Support a Loved One's Physical Healing

No matter how near or far a loved one may be, this simple charm can support and speed their healing process. (In the interest of free will, please be sure to ask their permission first.)

Ingredients
A bundle of dried white sage, with a dish to catch burning embers
A lighter or matches
A clear quartz point

On a Sunday when the sky is clear and the sun is high in the sky, light the sage so that it's smoking like incense. Purify the crystal by bathing it in the smoke. When this feels complete, extinguish the sage by running it under water or sealing it tightly in a jar.

Next, empower the crystal in the sunlight while holding it in your right, open palm. As you do so, feel deep love for the person you are helping heal, and see them in the bright light of perfect wellbeing. In your mind's eye and with your heart's wisdom, clearly sense and envision their harmonious alignment with the healing energies of the earth and cosmos. Believe wholeheartedly in their body's natural ability to heal. Fully expect them to make a complete and speedy recovery.

Give the crystal to your loved one, and counsel them to keep it nearby. If necessary, you can send it in the mail. (You can tell them as much or as little about its healing properties as you feel is appropriate to their level of receptivity.)

Heal an Old Emotional Wound

When we've healed our emotions around a past trauma, we become wiser and stronger than we otherwise could have been. If you know you have one or more unhealed emotional wounds, this is good news! Your awareness of the issue means you have the clarity you need in order to heal.

While you won't see results overnight, commitment to this slow and steady ritual will allow you to heal the pain and emerge into the bright light of empowerment and strength.

Ingredients

Rescue Remedy (available online and at most health food stores)

Essential oil of rose geranium

A mister of rose water

In the evening, on or just after the full moon, put four drops of Rescue Remedy and four drops of geranium oil in the mister with the rose water. Shake well.

Whatever you would like to heal, bring it to mind. Feel the pain and remember the trauma. As you do so, mist your energy field with the potion. Repeat this process every morning and every night until the next full moon. Make sure to shake it every time before you mist, and make more as needed.

Help Someone Through a Crisis

This ritual will lend magical support to a loved one, whether or not you are physically present to help them on a tangible level as well.

Ingredients

An Archangel Michael prayer candle (available at magical supply stores and online, or you can make your own)

Frankincense incense and holder

A lighter or matches

Light the candle and incense. Relax your body and quiet your mind as you take some deep breaths. Then say:

> Archangel Michael, beautiful, fiery, and steadfast, please attend [name of person you want to heal] and support him/her in all ways. May he/she emerge as he/she is in truth: strong, healthy, wise, and victorious. I see him/her in the light of this truth now, and I give thanks.

Allow the incense to safely burn all the way down. Allow the candle to burn for as long as you can attend to it, and then extinguish it. Relight it whenever you safely can, extinguishing as needed, until it has burned down all the way.

Get Rid of a Stubborn Health Issue

When you have a stubborn health issue—I don't care if it's genetic, or you slipped on the ice, or you caught it from your nephew—there is always (always!) an emotional issue underlying it. Heal the emotional issue, and it's highly likely that (a) the physical issue will finally respond to treatment, (b) you'll finally discover the proper way to treat it, or (c) it will suddenly clear up all on its own.

Ingredients

A natural hot spring—at a resort or in nature—where you can safely soak undisturbed (While I highly recommend visiting an actual hot spring, if it's too difficult to get to a hot spring at this time, a bath in your own tub with two cups of Epsom salt dissolved in it will do.)

A notebook and pen

Plenty of drinking water

Before soaking in the water, set the intention to get to the emotional heart of the physical issue. Call on Coventina, the Celtic goddess of healing waters, by saying:

Coventina, lady of sacred springs and healing waters, I honor you. Thank you for granting me profound insight and the courage to deeply heal.

Feel Coventina's healing presence arrive, and sense her infusing the water with her power. Then soak.

As you soak, consider the emotions connected to the health issue. How does it make you feel? Weak, confused, dirty, disempowered, angry, hurt, or ashamed? In what past issues and challenges might these emotions have originated? Maybe there's something you think didn't affect you, or something you think you already dealt with, that could use revisiting. Perhaps there's someone in your life you haven't been willing to find fault with, but toward whom you are actually harboring a lot of anger. Perhaps you have a story about what a great childhood you had, when really you felt lonely or scared a lot of the time. Whatever comes up, be willing to see it clearly and feel the feelings fully. Know that whatever you can feel, you can heal. You don't have to keep holding on to it forever, but first you have to know what it is.

Write down any clues, thoughts, or realizations in your journal, and commit to feeling all your feelings fully: to giving them the space, time, and attention they need in order for you to move through them.

Also write down any other insights you may have about your health habits or treatment options.

And, of course, make sure to stay hydrated while you soak!

18

Enhancing Your Magical Power

The magical spiritual path is an endless spiral. By walking it, you move deeper and deeper into the heart and soul of your power.

There may be times when it seems your power has fled, or when you question whether it was ever there to begin with. While most magical practitioners feel this way at one point or another, the truth is that your power never really leaves you. You may feel out of touch with it at times, but it's there, simply waiting for you to rediscover it.

It's also true that every experience—even if the experience causes you to feel disempowered, disenfranchised, and decidedly un-magical—ultimately moves you closer to magical mastery. Indeed, the long view will never fail to reveal that *every single occurrence* is a learning experience and an invitation to open up even more fully to the sumptuous splendor of your spiritual self.

The spells in this chapter will support you through the power portals along your spiritual and magical path, and facilitate the natural expansion of your gifts.

Find Your Magic

Perhaps you read the title of this chapter and thought, "Enhance my magical power? *What* magical power? I've never even found it in the first place!" Perhaps, deep down, you've never really felt confident that the magic is indeed within you. Well, my friend, this spell is for you.

Ingredients

A 78-card tarot deck with images you love

A robust cup of your favorite caffeinated beverage (or peppermint tea if caffeine doesn't agree with you)

A clear quartz crystal point

Separate the following twenty cards from the rest of the deck:

- The kings and queens of all suits (swords, cups, wands, and pentacles)
- The Fool
- The Magician
- The Priestess
- The Empress
- The Emperor
- The Hierophant
- Strength
- The Hermit
- The Star
- The Sun
- The Moon
- The World

Wake up before sunrise on the day of a full moon. With beverage (perhaps in a travel mug), crystal, and the twenty tarot cards in tow, find a good sunrise-viewing area outside where you feel safe and comfortable and where you won't be disturbed. A beach, balcony, park, hiking spot, or backyard area would all be good choices. (If you're a city dweller and you can't think of an appropriate spot nearby, you may want to do this during a vacation or weekend getaway.)

Settle in and sit comfortably. Relax your body and mind as you come fully into the moment.

As soon as the sun peeks visibly over the horizon, hold the crystal in your right hand and begin to enjoy your beverage. Fully take in the sun's spectacular early morning show as you think to yourself, "The sun is rising on my power." As the sun continues its ascent, know that your magical power is being awakened and illuminated.

Once the sun is over the horizon and you can see it in its entirety (and ideally once you've finished your drink), say or whisper:

Great Spirit, Great Holy Mystery, God / Goddess / All That Is,

Your magic is my magic. Your power is my power.

Your wisdom is my wisdom.

For this, I give thanks.

One with infinity, I am also unique in my expression within this mysterious dance of time.

Once these words have been spoken, immediately shuffle and then draw one of the cards. This card will be a mirror of your power as it is being expressed right now, through you. By looking at the image, get an intuitive feel for how this is true. There is no need to overly intellectualize: simply acknowledge that something significant about the card's energy is within you. Feel that something awakening and blossoming even more fully.

Then once again say:

One with infinity, I am also unique in my expression within this mysterious dance of time.

My power has been found. My power has been awakened.

For this, I give thanks.

Feel deep gratitude for this moment, for your connection with the Divine, and for your magical power. Stay with this for as long as it feels right.

Until the next full moon, keep the crystal and tarot card on your altar as a reminder and focal point for your newly discovered magic. As you study, meditate, and consult with your intuition, your understanding of the card (as it relates to your magic) will deepen over time.

Rediscover Your Magic

You were on fire. Your magical mojo was flowing and glowing like white-hot molten lava, until one day ... it wasn't.

If you're wondering where your magic went and how to get it back, this spell is for you.

Ingredients

Someplace *other than your home* where you can stay *by yourself* for at least *one full day* (one day and two nights)

At least a dozen roses of any color

One or more vases or jars

Clean, comfy pajamas you feel great in

At least one inspiring book to read (chosen for the joy of reading, not to enrich yourself)

Super-healthy, clean food to eat (like grains, beans, and whole fruits and vegetables)

Lots of clean drinking water

Your favorite coffee or tea (optional)

As noted in the list of ingredients, it's important for you to do this ritual somewhere other than your home where you can stay by yourself for at least one full day. This can be a campsite, a cabin, a guesthouse, the home of a friend or family member who is out of town, or even a hotel room.

When you get there, turn off your phone and put the roses in water, keeping them together or arranging them in different spots around the place. That evening, take a shower or bath and don the pajamas. Read the book until you get tired.

The next day, stay in your pajamas and do not turn on your phone for any reason. (If you need to warn people you'll be off the grid for a day, do so before you leave.) Also do not turn on your computer or watch any movies or television. This will be a screen-free day. At any time that you'd like some entertainment, you can do something like this:

- Go outside and watch the birds, clouds, and wind in the trees
- Read your book
- Drink a cup of coffee or tea
- Cook or bake something healthy to eat
- Take a shower or bath
- Give yourself a facial or paint your nails

- Meditate
- Do yoga
- Smell or gaze at the roses
- Put on music and dance (provided you can do so without turning on your phone)

If boredom or loneliness starts to creep in, let it. Breathe into the feeling and uncover the emotions behind it. If sadness or anger arises, let it. If distressed thoughts crowd into your mind, listen to them. Resist nothing. Keep breathing and allowing and feeling as much as you possibly can. (Of course, relaxing by yourself for a day may also bring nothing but joy!)

After sunset, strew rose petals on the floor to create a magic circle. Sit inside it comfortably, with your spine relatively straight. Relax, center yourself, and breathe deeply. When you feel ready, say:

I honor myself. I honor my feelings. I honor my thoughts. I love myself. I take very good care of myself. I give myself time and space to be me. I know just what is best for me, and I take action on that knowledge immediately. I trust that everything I need is available to me and arrives in perfect timing. I am brave. I am a divine child. I have divine support. I am never alone. I am always powerful and backed by divine power. I now reclaim the power that is mine by divine right.

Feel and know that all you have said is true. Repeat it if you'd like. Continue to sit in the circle until the energy you've raised feels like it has reached a crescendo. Then say:

God/Goddess/All That Is, thank you for my magic.

Infinite intelligence, thank you for my magic.

Divine helpers, thank you for my magic.

Thank you for my magic, thank you for my magic,
thank you for my magic.

Thank you, thank you, thank you.

Blessed be. And so it is.

Place the rose petals on the earth or in a yard waste or compost bin. For the remainder of the evening, continue to keep your phone and all screens turned off. Spend your time relaxing quietly or engaging in any of the suggested activities. Continue to allow all of your thoughts and feelings to be exactly as they are. Then, when you're ready, go to sleep.

Maximize Your Manifestation Ability

Our ability to magnetize magic and miracles depends on many factors, such as our level of energetic harmony and potency, our degree of trust in divine orchestration, and our ability to clearly focus our thoughts and feelings on what we'd like to experience. This potion cultivates all these factors and more. By the end of the moon cycle, you'll have majorly multiplied your manifesting mojo.

Ingredients
A clean blue water bottle you love (Glass or plastic will both work.)
Drinking water
Kunzite gem essence (available at AlaskanEssences.com)

On the morning of a new moon, fill your bottle with drinking water. Add two drops of kunzite essence and drink. (You can drink it all at once or sip it throughout the day, as long as you finish it all.) Repeat every day until the next new moon.

Enhance Your Personal Power

Potent personal power translates to charisma, confidence, and general life mastery. It means you stand your ground, speak your truth, enjoy your life, and feel comfortable in your own skin.

Ingredient
A hiking trail somewhere with trees

Simply go for a solitary walk on a beautiful nature trail. Keep your phone off and pay close attention to the trees, the feel of your feet on the earth, and all the other sensory treats that surround you. As you walk, feel that you are absorbing strength and beauty from your surroundings.

I know this spell sounds so simple that it almost doesn't sound like a spell at all, but every time you do it, your personal power will enjoy a significant boost.

Supercharge Your Luck

You are naturally lucky. Tapping into that luck is like finding your groove on a dance floor: once you've got it, you've got it. And it gains more exuberance and enthusiasm with each new song.

Those of us dancing to the rhythm of luck seem to easily attract everything, from parking places to happy coincidences to life partners, all like it's the natural way of the world.

This charm will help you find your luck if it's missing, or increase it if it's already there.

Ingredients
1 acorn

1 tablespoon dried elecampane root

A square of bright red cotton cloth

Hemp twine

Essential oil of lavender

On a Sunday when the moon is waxing, place the acorn and elecampane on the cloth and tie it into a bundle with the twine to
create a charm. Anoint it with essential oil of lavender. Hold the
charm in your open, right palm and say:

> *I'm lucky yesterday, tomorrow, and today.*
> *I'm lucky at work and lucky at play.*
> *For this infinite luck that money can't buy,*
> *I thank water and earth, fire and sky.*

Keep the charm against your skin (perhaps safety-pinned to the
inside of your clothes) for seven days. Each day before you wear
it, reanoint it with the lavender oil and repeat the chant. After the
seven days, release the contents of the charm to the earth and
throw away the cloth and hemp twine.

Conclusion

I hope you've enjoyed this initiation into your magic. I've certainly enjoyed being your guide. May all you've learned and uncovered serve you well on your spiraling spiritual path. May your magical awareness and power ever increase. May you be a sparkling torch that illuminates and ignites the magic in others. And may you always remember that your very presence bring rays of grace and beauty to the world.

Brightest blessings, magical one. Now go forth and shine.

Bibliography

Chiorazzi, Anthony. "The Spirituality of Africa." *Harvard Gazette*, October 6, 2015. www.news.harvard.edu/gazette /story/2015/10/the-spirituality-of-africa. Interview with Jacob Olupona.

Collins, Terah Kathryn. *The Western Guide to Feng Shui: Creating Balance, Harmony, and Prosperity in Your Environment.* Carlsbad, CA: Hay House, 1996.

Cunningham, Scott. *Wicca: A Guide for the Solitary Practitioner.* St. Paul, MN: Llewellyn, 1988.

Dugan, Ellen. *Practical Protection Magick: Guarding & Reclaiming Your Power.* Woodbury, MN: Llewellyn, 2011.

———. *The Witches Tarot.* Woodbury, MN: Llewellyn, 2012.

Hartfield, Angela. *Whispers of Lord Ganesha.* Glen Waverley, VIC, Australia: Blue Angel Publishing, 2016. Distributed by Llewellyn.

Hendricks, Gay. *The Big Leap: Conquer Your Hidden Fear and Take Life to the Next Level.* New York: HarperCollins, 2009.

Illes, Judika. *The Element Encyclopedia of 5000 Spells*. London: Harper Element, 2004.

————. *Encyclopedia of Mystics, Saints & Sages: A Guide to Asking for Protection, Wealth, Happiness, and Everything Else!* New York: HarperCollins, 2011.

Judith, Anodea. *Chakras: Seven Keys to Awakening and Healing the Energy Body*. Carlsbad, CA: Hay House, 2016.

Karcher, Stephen. *Total I Ching: Myths for Change*. London: Time Warner, 2003.

Kempton, Sally. *Awakening Shakti: The Transformative Power of the Goddesses of Yoga*. Boulder, CO: Sounds True, 2013.

Kirsch, Jonathan. *God Against the Gods: The History of the War Between Monotheism and Polytheism*. New York: Penguin, 2004.

————. *The Grand Inquisitor's Manual: A History of Terror in the Name of God*. New York: HarperCollins, 2008.

Kondo, Marie. *The Life-Changing Magic of Tidying Up: The Japanese Art of Decluttering and Organizing*. Berkeley, CA: Ten Speed Press, 2014.

László, Ervin. *Science and the Akashic Field: An Integral Theory of Everything*. Rochester, VT: Inner Traditions, 2004.

Linn, Denise. *Altars: Bringing Sacred Shrines into Your Everyday Life*. New York: Wellspring/Ballantine, 1999.

————. *Past Lives, Present Miracles*. Carlsbad, CA: Hay House, 2008.

Lynch, David. *Catching the Big Fish: Meditation, Consciousness, and Creativity*. New York: Penguin, 2006.

Melody. *Love Is in the Earth: A Kaleidoscope of Crystals*. Wheat Ridge, CO: Earth-Love Publishing House, 1995.

Mitchell, Stephen, trans. *Tao Te Ching: A New English Version*. New York: Harper & Row, 1988.

Pujari, R. M., Pradeep Kolhe, and N. R. Kumar, eds. *Pride of India*. New Delhi, India: Samskrita Bharati, 2006.

Schiff, Stacy. *The Witches: Suspicion, Betrayal, and Hysteria in 1692 Salem*. New York: Hachette Book Group, 2015.

Shinn, Florence Scovel. *The Game of Life and How to Play It*. 1925; reprint, New York: Tribeca Books, 2010.

Shroder, Tom. *Old Souls: Compelling Evidence from Children Who Remember Past Lives*. New York: Fireside, 1999.

Schrödinger, Erwin. *My View of the World*. Cambridge, England: Cambridge University Press, 1964.

Starhawk. *The Spiral Dance: A Rebirth of the Ancient Religion of the Great Goddess*. San Francisco, CA: Harper & Row, 1979.

Virtue, Doreen. *Angel Therapy: Healing Messages for Every Area of Your Life*. Carlsbad, CA: Hay House, 1997.

———. *Divine Magic: The Seven Sacred Secrets of Manifestation*. Carlsbad, CA: Hay House, 2006.

———. *Goddess Guidance Oracle Cards*. Carlsbad, CA: Hay House, 2004.

Whitehurst, Tess. *The Good Energy Book: Creating Harmony and Balance for Yourself and Your Home*. Woodbury, MN: Llewellyn, 2012.

———. *Magic of Flowers Oracle*. Woodbury, MN: Llewellyn, 2015.

Woolfolk, Joanna Martine. *The Only Astrology Book You'll Ever Need*. Lanham, MD: Madison Books, 2001.

Acknowledgments

Thank you, Great Holy Mystery.

Elysia Gallo and Andrea Neff, thank you for (over and over again) making me appear smarter and more articulate than I actually am. Sandra Weschcke, Bill Krause, and everyone at Llewellyn, thank you for holding a space where the magical thinkers of the world thrive and feel at home. Brandi Palechek, thank you for being my social media and online strategizing superhero. Good Vibe Tribe members and Divine Resonance Magic practitioners, thank you for being such truly fabulous magic workers and for teaching me so much. Sacred Circle of Fairydust and Ashes, thank you for all our laughter-filled pagan family gatherings. Mom, thank you for the letter, and for everything you wrote in it. Ted Bruner, thank you for being my co-creator in so many things, including our dear, cozy, remarkable life way up in the mountains that I love so much.

Thank you, thank you, thank you.

To Write to the Author

If you wish to contact the author or would like more information about this book, please write to the author in care of Llewellyn Worldwide Ltd. and we will forward your request. Both the author and the publisher appreciate hearing from you and learning of your enjoyment of this book and how it has helped you. Llewellyn Worldwide Ltd. cannot guarantee that every letter written to the author can be answered, but all will be forwarded. Please write to:

Tess Whitehurst
℅ Llewellyn Worldwide
2143 Wooddale Drive
Woodbury, MN 55125-2989

Please enclose a self-addressed stamped envelope for reply,
or $1.00 to cover costs. If outside the U.S.A., enclose
an international postal reply coupon.

Many of Llewellyn's authors have websites with additional information and resources. For more information, please visit our website at www.llewellyn.com.

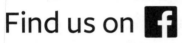 

Simple Charms
& Practical Tips for
Creating a Harmonious Home

MAGICAL
HOUSEKEEPING

Tess Whitehurst

Magical Housekeeping
Simple Charms and Practical Tips
for Creating a Harmonious Home
TESS WHITEHURST

Every inch and component of your home is filled with an invisible life force and unique magical energy. *Magical Housekeeping* teaches readers how to sense, change, channel, and direct these energies to create harmony in their homes, joy in their hearts, and success in all areas of their lives.

In this engaging guide, energy consultant and teacher Tess Whitehurst shares her secrets for creating an energetically powerful and positive home. Written for those new to metaphysics as well as experienced magical practitioners, *Magical Housekeeping* will teach readers how to summon success, happiness, romance, abundance, and all the desires of the heart. And, by guiding them to make changes in both the seen and unseen worlds simultaneously, this dynamic and delightful book will help to activate and enhance readers' intuition and innate magical power.

978-0-7387-1985-6, 240 pp., 5³⁄₁₆ x 8　　　　　　**$16.95**
